Learn Chinese Radicals:
Writing Practice Book

Chinese for Beginners

SCHOEMAN A.D. | 王哲洋

Copyright © 2019 Daniel Schoeman
All rights reserved.
ISBN 978-0-7961-6426-1
Second Edition

CONTENTS

Introduction: The Basics Of Chinese Radicals......................05

1. What Are Chinese Radicals?...01

2. What Is Their Function..05

3. Is It Necessary To Learn These Radicals?.......................09

4. Is It Necessary To Practice Radicals For Writing?.........17

5. A General List Of All 214 Radicals..................................21

6. Writing Chinese Radicals...14

7. How To Write..15

8. How To Use This Book...17

9. Practice Radicals...18

10. Typical Characters & Self Practice.................................54

DISCLAIMER

PLEASE NOTE! This is a book to practice the 214 standard Chinese radicals in.

The list provided is 100% correct, but Chinese radical lists found online can vary due to several factors:

- **Historical Variations:** Throughout history, there have been different categorizations and interpretations of radicals, leading to variations in radical lists.
- **Simplification and Standardization:** The Chinese writing system has undergone reforms, such as simplification in mainland China and traditional forms in Taiwan and Hong Kong. These reforms may result in different radical lists being used in different regions.
- **Scholarly Interpretations:** Different scholars may have different perspectives on which components should be considered radicals, leading to variations in radical lists.
- **Educational Curriculum:** Radical lists used in educational materials may be tailored to suit the specific needs of learners or the requirements of the curriculum, resulting in variations.
- **Usage and Frequency:** Some lists may prioritize radicals based on their frequency of use or importance in understanding characters, leading to variations depending on the purpose of the list.

Overall, the variation in Chinese radical lists reflects the complexity and richness of the Chinese writing system, as well as the diverse perspectives and needs of learners and users.

Radicals serve as headers in dictionaries, organizing characters or words. The 214 Kangxi radicals specifically categorize entries in the Kangxi dictionary; they are not universally employed in other dictionaries, unless another dictionary deliberately adopts the same radical set. Consequently, if a smaller dictionary opts not to include some obscure characters found in larger or more comprehensive dictionaries, it may lack the complete set of Kangxi radicals.

The Kangxi dictionary, being Traditional Chinese, uses its distinct set of radicals, which differs from those used in Simplified Chinese dictionaries. However, entries in Simplified Chinese dictionaries may still be rooted in the Kangxi dictionary.

Radicals, whether Kangxi or otherwise, are essentially arbitrary. They often bear little relation to a character's meaning or pronunciation. Therefore, it's entirely acceptable for a new dictionary publisher to devise their own radical system for character grouping.

The Basics Of Chinese Radicals

What Are Chinese Radicals?

Chinese radicals are components of Chinese characters that are used to organize and index the characters in dictionaries. They are essentially the building blocks of Chinese characters and often carry meaning or contribute to the pronunciation of the character.

The following is an analysis from AciaSociety.org:

"Traditional Chinese groups all characters according to 214 radicals (Simplified uses 189), which are organized based on number of strokes into a chart called the bushou. Each radical is itself a freestanding character-word, such as one, woman, child, cliff, field, tree, millet, halberd, leather, and bird."

Learning Chinese radicals can be extremely beneficial for several reasons:

- **Understanding Character Structure:** Radicals provide insight into the structure of Chinese characters, helping learners recognize recurring patterns and components. This understanding makes it easier to remember characters and guess the meanings or pronunciations of unfamiliar ones.

- **Building Vocabulary:** By learning radicals, you effectively learn the building blocks of many characters. This knowledge can help you decipher the meaning and pronunciation of new characters based on their radical components, even if you've never encountered them before.

- **Using Dictionaries:** Many Chinese dictionaries organize characters by their radicals. Knowing radicals allows you to navigate these dictionaries efficiently, making it easier to look up unfamiliar characters and expand your vocabulary.

- **Writing Characters:** Understanding radicals can also aid in writing Chinese characters. By breaking characters down into their radical components, you can tackle the task of writing characters more systematically.

- **Cultural Understanding:** Chinese radicals often carry cultural or historical significance. Learning about radicals can provide insights into Chinese culture, as many radicals are derived from pictographs or ideographs representing objects, concepts, or cultural elements.

What Is Their Function?

Radicals are typically either *semantic* or *phonetic*.
Semantic radicals convey meaning, providing clues about the general category or concept associated with a character.
Phonetic radicals, on the other hand, give clues about the pronunciation of the character.

Example of Meaning (semantic):
The Chinese character component 女 (nǔ) signifies "woman." When you see this component within another character, it typically indicates that the character is connected to women in some manner. Therefore, if we look at 妈妈 (māma) we can see that the 女 (nǔ) component serves as a clue, telling us that this character represents a female, a mother!

Example of Pronunciation (phonetic):
The Chinese character 爸 (bà) indicates "father". It is a character that consists of the 父 (fù) component at the top (the semantic component), which means "father", and the bottom component 巴 (bā) which helps you with the pronunciation.

Is It Necessary To Learn These Radicals?

While it's not absolutely necessary to learn radicals to speak Chinese conversationally, mastering them can significantly enhance your ability to read, write, and understand Chinese characters. It's a valuable investment for anyone serious about learning the language.

A classic example:
The character 家 (jiā) – **home** is made up of 宀 (mián) – **roof** and 豕 (shǐ) – **pig**. In ancient China, pigs were commonly housed indoors.
The presence of a pig in a house signified human habitation, making it clear that the house was indeed someone's residence.

Take note that radicals don't consistently provide reliable assistance. In numerous cases, a radical may not offer any significant clues regarding the meaning or pronunciation, thus it's wise to proceed cautiously.
While radicals can sometimes be helpful, they're not infallible allies and shouldn't be blindly trusted!

Is It Necessary To Practice Radicals For Writing?

Yes!!! It is definitely necessary to practice writing all of the radicals. Radicals are the building blocks of Chinese characters, and understanding them can help you recognize patterns and meanings within characters. By familiarizing yourself with radicals, you'll have a better grasp of how characters are constructed, which can aid you in both writing and understanding Chinese.

A General List Of All 214 Chinese Radicals And Their Meaning:

RADICAL #	RADICAL	PINYIN	MEANING
1	一	yī	One
2	丨	gǔn	Line
3	丶	zhǔ	Dot
4	丿 乀 ㇇	piě	Slash
5	乙 乚	yǐ	Second
6	亅	jué	Hook
7	二	èr	Two
8	亠	tóu	Lid
9	人 亻	rén	Person
10	儿	rén	Legs
11	入	rù	Enter
12	八 丷	bā	Eight
13	冂	jiōng	Down box
14	冖	mì	Cover
15	冫	bīng	Ice
16	几	jǐ	Table
17	凵	qiǎn	Open box
18	刂 ㇌ 刀	dāo	Knife
19	力	lì	Power
20	勹	bāo	Wrap
21	匕	bǐ	Ladle/Dagger
22	匚	fāng	Right open box

23	匸	xì	Hiding enclosure
24	十	shí	Ten
25	卜	bǔ	Divination
26	卩	jié	Seal/Joint
27	厂	hǎn	Cliff/House
28	厶	mǒu/sī	Private
29	又	yòu	Again
30	口	kǒu	Mouth
31	囗	wéi	Enclosure
32	土	tǔ	Earth
33	士	shì	Scholar
34	夂	zhǐ	Go
35	夊	suī	Go slowly
36	夕	xī	Night
37	大	dà	Big
38	女	nǚ	Woman
39	子	zǐ	Child
40	宀	mián	Roof
41	寸	cùn	Inch
42	小 ⺌ ⺍	xiǎo	Small
43	尢	wāng	Lame
44	尸	shī	Corpse
45	屮	chè	Sprout
46	山	shān	Mountain
47	川 巛	chuān	River
48	工	gōng	Work
49	己	jǐ	Oneself
50	巾	jīn	Towel
51	干	gān/gàn	Dry/Do
52	幺	yāo	Youngest
53	广	guǎng	Shelter
54	廴	yǐn	Stride
55	廾	gǒng	Hands joined

56	弋	yì	Shoot with a bow
57	弓	gōng	Bow
58	彐彑	jì	Snout
59	彡	shān	Hair
60	彳	chì	Step
61	心忄	xīn	Heart
62	戈	gē	Spear
63	戶户	hù	Door
64	扌	shǒu	Hand
65	支	zhī	Branch
66	攴攵	pū	Rap/Beat
67	文	wén	Script
68	斗	dǒu	Vessel
69	斤	jīn	Axe
70	方	fāng	Square
71	无/旡	wú/jì	Not/Choke on something eaten
72	日	rì	Sun
73	曰	yuē	Say
74	月	yuè	Moon
75	木朩	mù	Tree
76	欠	qiàn	Lack
77	止	zhǐ	Stop
78	歹	dǎi	Death
79	殳	shū	Weapon
80	母	mǔ	Mother
81	比	bǐ	Compare
82	毛	máo	Fur
83	氏	shì	Clan
84	气	qì	Steam
85	水氵氺	shuǐ	Water
86	火灬	huǒ	Fire
87	爪爫	zhǎo/zhuā	Claw

88	父	fù	Father
89	爻	yáo	Lines on a trigram
90	丬	pán	Half of a tree trunk
91	片	qiáng	Slice
92	牙	yá	Tooth
93	牛 牛 牜	niú	Cow
94	犬 犭	quǎn	Dog
95	玄	xuán	Profound
96	王 玉	wáng/yù	King/Jade
97	瓜	guā	Melon
98	瓦	wǎ	Tile
99	甘	gān	Sweet
100	生	shēng	Life
101	用	yòng	Use
102	田	tián	Field
103	疋 正	pǐ	Foot
104	疒	nè	Sick
105	癶	bō	Unbalanced footsteps
106	白	bái	White
107	皮	pí	Skin
108	皿	mǐn	Dish
109	目	mù	Eye
110	矛	máo	Spear
111	矢	shǐ	Arrow
112	石	shí	Stone
113	示 礻	shì	Spirit
114	禸	róu	Rub
115	禾	hé	Grain
116	穴	xué	Cave
117	立	lì	Stand
118	竹 ⺮ ケ	zhú	Bamboo
119	米	mǐ	Rice

120	糸 纟	sī	Silk
121	缶	fǒu	Jar
122	网 罒 冈	wǎng	Net
123	羊 ⺶ ⺷	yáng	Sheep
124	羽	yǔ	Feather
125	老 耂	lǎo	Old
126	而	ér	And
127	耒	lěi	Plaw
128	耳	ěr	Ear
129	聿	yù	Brush
130	肉 月	ròu	Meat
131	臣	chén	Minister
132	自	zì	Oneself
133	至	zhì	Arrive
134	臼	jiù	Mortar
135	舌	shé	Tongue
136	舛	chuǎn	Contrary
137	舟	zhōu	Boat
138	艮	gèn	Mountain
139	色	sè	Color
140	艹	cǎo	Grass
141	虍	hū	Stripes on a tiger
142	虫	chóng	Insect
143	血	xuè	Blood
144	行	xíng	Walk
145	衣 衤	yī	Clothes
146	襾	yà	Cover
147	见	jiàn	See
148	角	jiǎo	Horn
149	讠	yán	Speech
150	谷	gǔ	Valley
151	豆	dòu	Bean
152	豕	shǐ	Pig

153	豸	zhì	Legless insect
154	贝	bèi	Shell
155	赤	chì	Red
156	走	zǒu	Walk
157	足	zú	Foot
158	身	shēn	Body
159	车	chē	Cart
160	辛	xīn	Bitter
161	辰	chén	Day time
162	辶	chuò	Walk
163	邑 阝	yì	City
164	酉	yǒu	Wine vessel
165	采	biàn	Distinguish
166	里	lǐ	Village/Unit of distance
167	金 钅	jīn	Metal
168	长	cháng	Long
169	门	mén	Gate
170	阜 阝	fù	Mound
171	隶	lì	Slave
172	隹	zhuī	Short-tailed bird
173	雨	yǔ	Rain
174	青	qīng	Blue/Green
175	非	fēi	Wrong
176	面	miàn	Face
177	革	gé	Leather
178	韦	wěi	Soft leather
179	韭	jiǔ	Leek
180	音	yīn	Sound
181	页	yè	Page
182	风	fēng	Wind
183	飞	fēi	Fly
184	食 饣	shí	Eat

185	首	shǒu	Head
186	香	xiāng	Fragrant
187	马	mǎ	Horse
188	骨	gǔ	Bone
189	高	gāo	High
190	髟	biāo	Long hair
191	门/鬥	mén/dòu	Fight
192	鬯	chàng	Sacrificial wine
193	鬲	lì	Cauldron
194	鬼	guǐ	Ghost
195	鱼	yú	Fish
196	鸟	niǎo	Bird
197	卤	lǔ	Brine
198	鹿	lù	Deer
199	麦	mài	Wheat
200	麻	má	Hemp
201	黄	huáng	Yellow
202	黍	shǔ	Millet
203	黑	hēi	Black
204	黹	zhǐ	Embroidery
205	黾	měng	Frog
206	鼎	dǐng	Tripod
207	鼓	gǔ	Drum
208	鼠	shǔ	Rat
209	鼻	bí	Nose
210	齐	qí	Neat
211	齿	chǐ	Tooth
212	龙	lóng	Dragon
213	龟	guī	Turtle
214	龠	yuè	Flute

Next, let's examine what's involved in the "writing" of Chinese characters and how to approach character writing correctly.

Writing Chinese Radicals

This book is dedicated to the writing of characters, specifically Chinese radicals.

If you look closely at the two Chinese words displayed on this page, you will see small numbers scattered around each character.
These numbers are stroke numbers and they represent one completed stroke, as drawn with a calligraphy pen.
We call them the **Stroke Order** of the character.

The concept of a numbered "stroke order" is to help the student to write the character by following the correct sequential order.
These stroke orders help you to acquire appropriate habits early on and to avoid making typical beginner mistakes.
Keep characters uniform in size (and position) and use the guide (grid) to assist you.

How to Write

At first glance, the grouping of strokes within a character might seem just plain random and disorganized; this is a normal reaction that every new student of Mandarin will experience.

If we look a bit deeper, we see that there is definitely a natural order present, which allows the brush to move and flow in an elegant, effortless motion.

Let's look at the following diagram provided.
It presents us with the **layout of the stroke order of a character.**

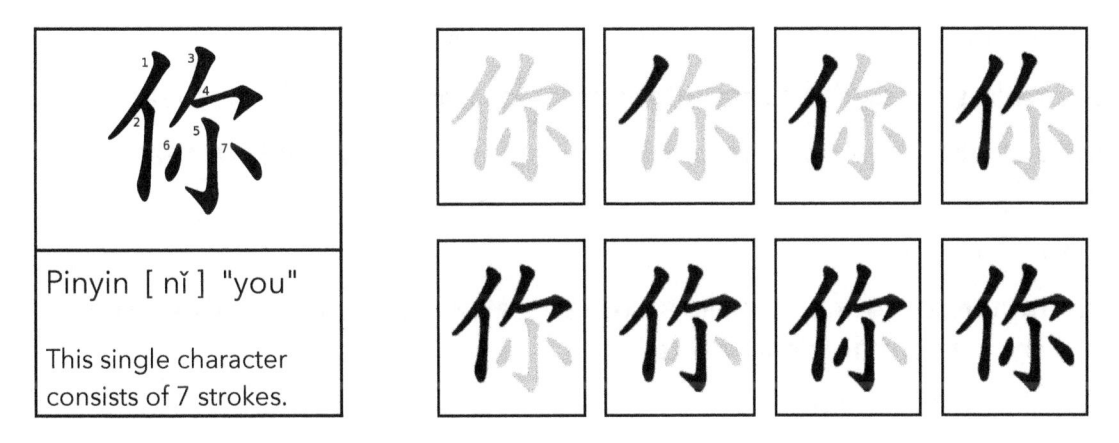

Pinyin [nǐ] "you"

This single character consists of 7 strokes.

Chinese characters consist of pictures or symbols.
When we *write* characters, we are actually *drawing*.
(Traditionally, a brush is used for calligraphy, but of course every stroke can also be drawn with a pen or a pencil.)

An individual character represents a single *syllable*.
A word can consist of one, two or more syllables.

Many characters consist of a graphical component called a *radical*.
This radical helps to identify the *meaning* of the character.
Radicals are often found on the left side of the character.
In the example provided, we notice that the character for "you" can be divided into the following components:

亻 + 尔 = 你

The radical on the left 亻 means "man", as in a *person*.
Knowing the radical helps us to identify the word and to comprehend its meaning.

Always keep an eye out for radicals when introduced to new characters.
Knowing the radical, helps us to identify and to memorize the character.

Look at the character diagram provided on the previous page.

To write characters, we follow a simple yet specific order:

1. Top to bottom.

Stroke 1, before Stroke 2.

2. Left to right.

Stroke 1+2 completed the "person" radical. It is completed before the rest of the character on the right.

3. Upper left corner to lower right corner.

Stroke 3 - Stroke 7

4. Outside to inside.

This is normally for characters with "boxes". The box is drawn first.

5. When two strokes cross, the horizontal stroke is drawn first. The vertical last.

6. With slanted strokes, the slanting stroke to the left is drawn before the one slanting to the right.

Stroke 1 before Stroke 2.

7. When a character component looks symmetrical, we draw the center stroke first, followed by the symmetrical wings.

Stroke 5 first, followed by 6 and 7.

The secret to writing characters is practice.
1. Look at the character.
2. Dissect it by looking at the recognizable radicals and components present.
3. Write it down as many times as possible on Chinese writing paper.
4. Remember to stay within the margins of the boxes provided and to keep characters uniform in size.

Conclusion

a. These are the basic writing guidelines to be followed as they apply to all Chinese characters.
b. Start with a simple character, follow the stroke order sequence and notice that

your pen is flowing from *top to bottom* and *left to right*. This sequence should become second nature with all students who want to excel at writing.

c. Take note that these seven rules are in place to help you become more efficient at writing. This is where practice will make the difference.

d. Not all seven steps will apply to all characters; some characters are simple in make-up, and others are more complicated.

How To Use This Book

Practice, practice and practice some more. Write every radical as many times as is needed, and build muscle memory till writing becomes second nature to you.

We provide you with:

- A list of more than 200 radicals (Traditional and Simplified characters) that you should practice as often as possible. Variants of the characters are also provided.
- The meaning of the radical in English.
- The pronunciation of the radical in PinYin.
- The stroke count of the radical. The most obvious difference between Traditional Chinese and Simplified Chinese is the way that the characters look. Traditional characters are typically more complicated and have more strokes, while simplified characters are, as the name suggests, simpler and have fewer strokes. As a student of Mandarin you should always pay attention to the stroke order and stroke count of the characters.

Table Legend:

(V) - Variant

(T) - Traditional Character

* - Only used in Traditional Characters

Unmarked forms are the normal Simplified Chinese version.

Practice Radicals

yī one 1 Stroke	一								
shù/gǔn line 1 Stroke	丨								
zhǔ/diǎn dot 1 Stroke	丶								
piě slash 1 Stroke	丿	㇏ (V)	㇌ (V)						
yǐ second 1 Stroke	乙	ㄣ (V)	ㄱ (V)						
jué/gōu hook 1 Stroke	亅								
èr two 2 Strokes	二								
tóu lid 2 Strokes	亠								
rén man 2 Strokes	人	亻 (V)							
ér son, child, legs 2 Strokes	儿								
rù enter 2 Strokes	入								
bā eight 2 Strokes	八	丷 (V)							

Self Practice

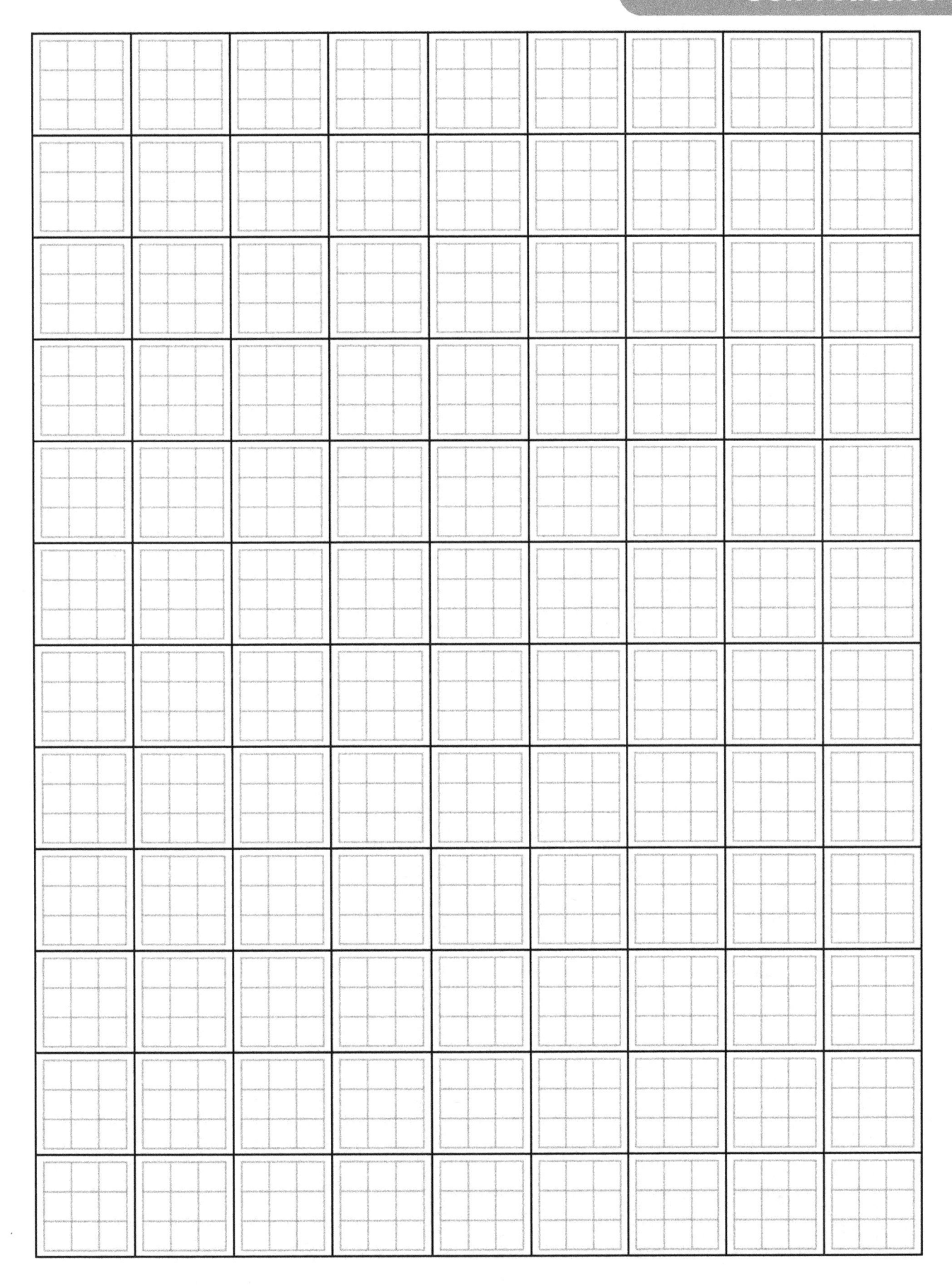

Practice Radicals

jiōng wide 2 Strokes	冂							
mì cloth cover 2 Strokes	冖							
bīng ice 2 Stroke	冫							
jī/ jǐ table, several 2 Strokes	几							
kǎn/ qiǎn receptacle 2 Strokes	凵							
dāo knife 2 Strokes	刀	刂 (V)	刁 (V)					
lì power 2 Strokes	力							
bāo wrap 2 Strokes	勹							
bǐ/pìn spoon 2 Strokes	匕							
fāng box 2 Strokes	匚							
xǐ/xì hiding enclosure 2 Strokes	匸							
shí ten 2 Strokes	十							

Self Practice

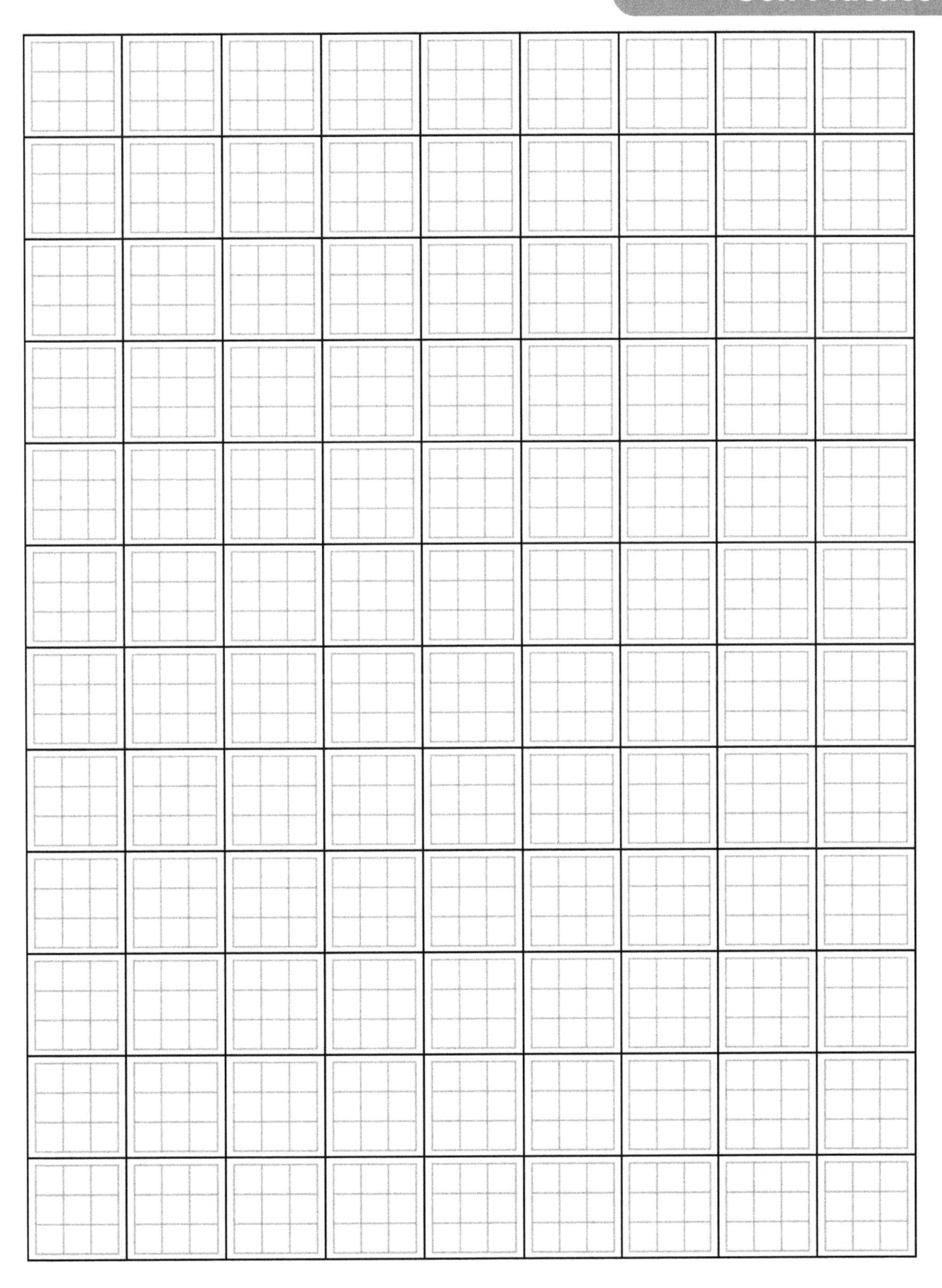

Practice Radicals

bǔ divination 2 Strokes	卜								
jié seal 2 Strokes	卩	㔾 (V)							
hǎn cliff 2 Strokes	厂								
sī/mǒu private 2 Strokes	厶								
yòu again 2 Strokes	又								
kǒu mouth 3 Strokes	口								
wéi enclosure 3 Strokes	囗								
tǔ earth 3 Strokes	土								
shì scholar 3 Strokes	士								
zhǐ go 3 Strokes	夂								
suī go slowly 3 Strokes	夊								
xī evening 3 Strokes	夕								

Self Practice

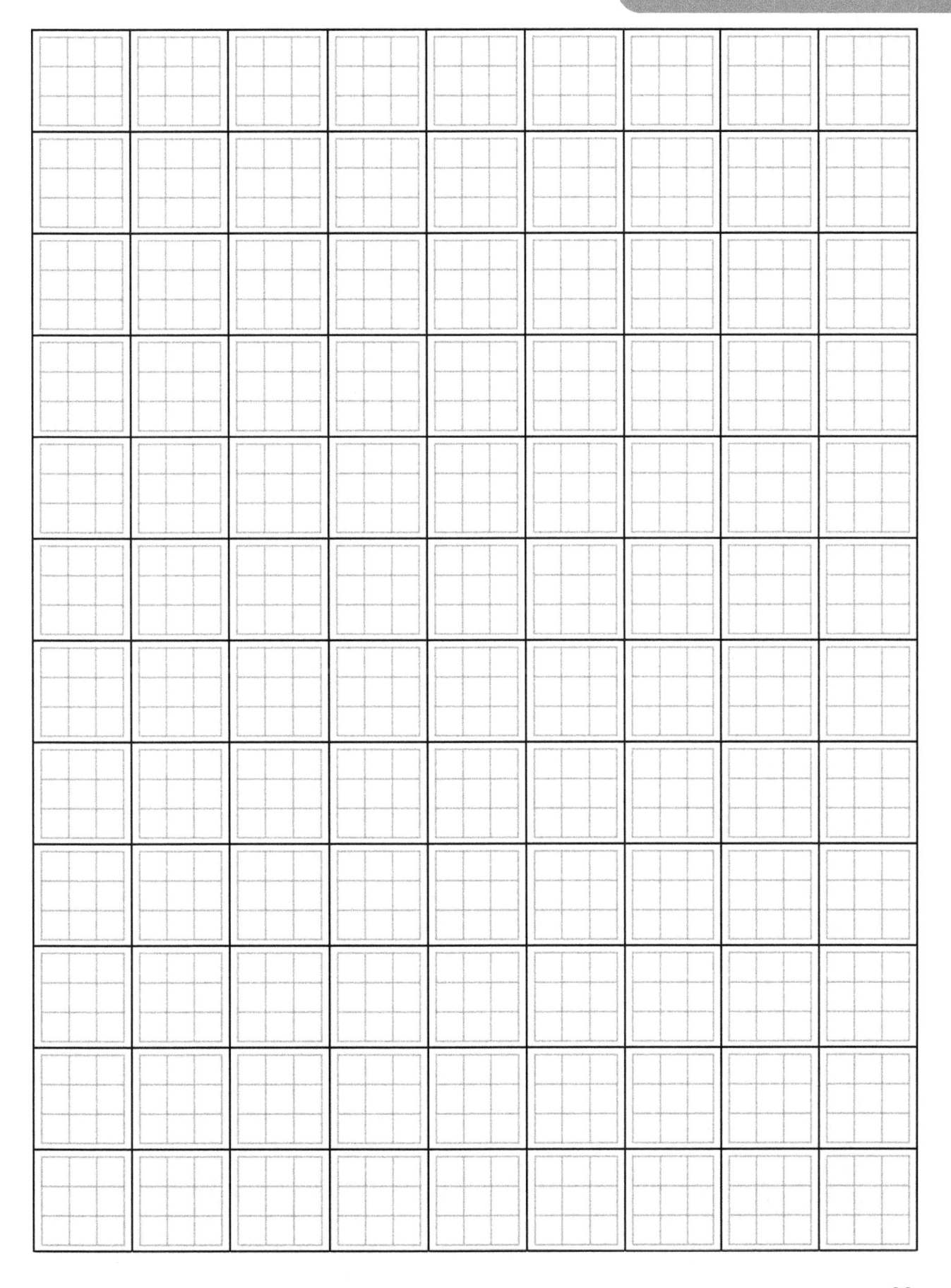

Practice Radicals

dà big, 3 Strokes	大	
nǚ woman, 3 Strokes	女	
zǐ child, 3 Strokes	子	
mián/ gài roof, 3 Strokes	宀	
cùn inch, 3 Strokes	寸	
xiǎo small, 3 Strokes	小	丷 (V) ⺌ (V)
wāng lame, 3 Strokes	尢	尣 (V)
shī corpse, 3 Strokes	尸	
chè sprout, 3 Strokes	屮	
shān mountain, 3 Strokes	山	
chuān river, 3 Strokes	川	巛 (V)
gōng work, 3 Strokes	工	

24

Self Practice

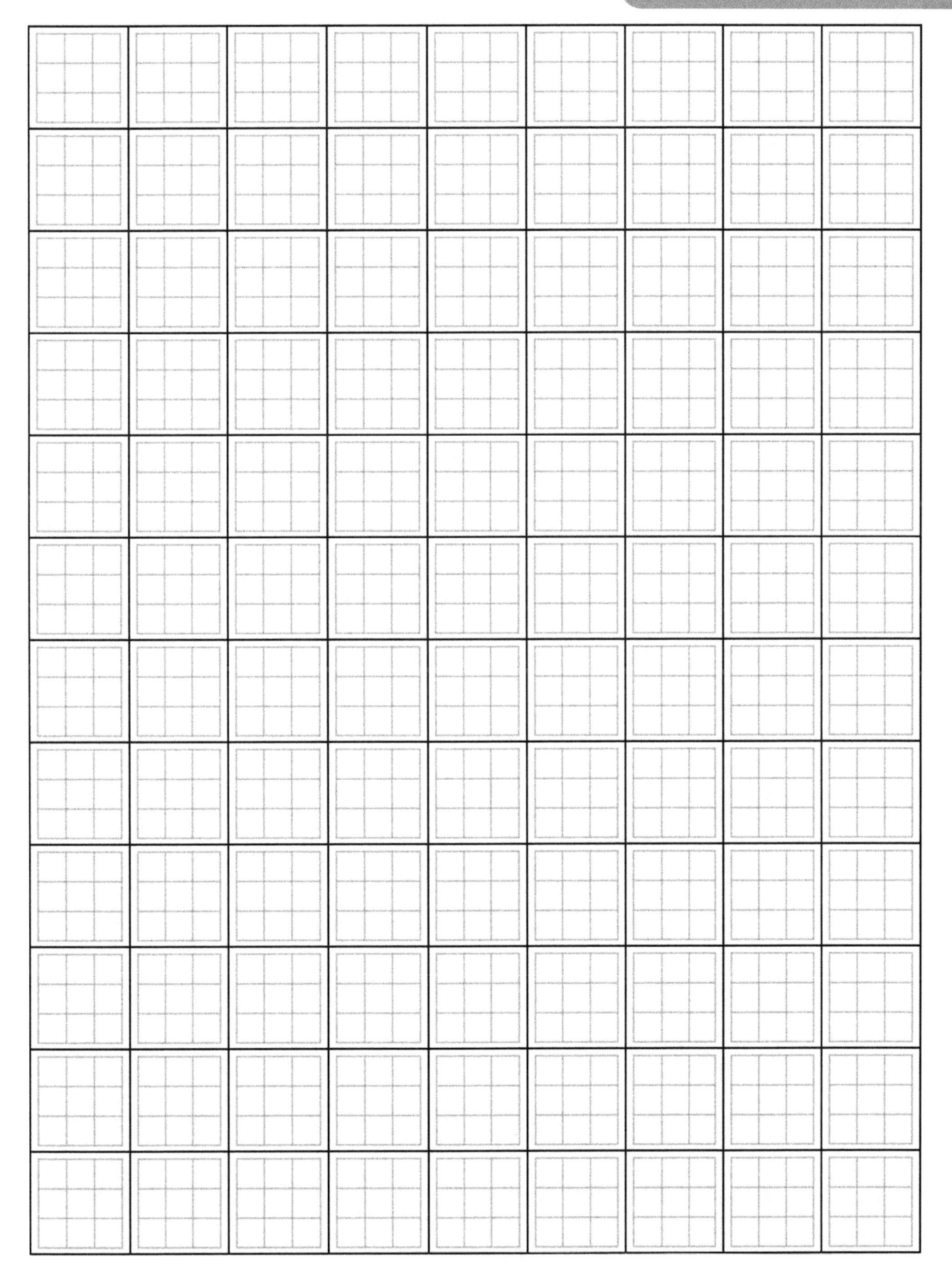

Practice Radicals

jǐ oneself 3 Strokes	己								
jīn turban 3 Strokes	巾								
gān/gàn dry 3 Strokes	干								
yāo short 3 Strokes	幺	么 (V)							
guǎng house on cliff 3 Strokes	广								
yǐn long stride 3 Stroke	廴								
gǒng hands, two 3 Strokes	廾								
yì shoot 3 Strokes	弋								
gōng bow 3 Strokes	弓								
jì snout 3 Strokes	彐	彑 (V)							
shān bristle 3 Strokes	彡								
chì step 3 Strokes	彳								

26

Self Practice

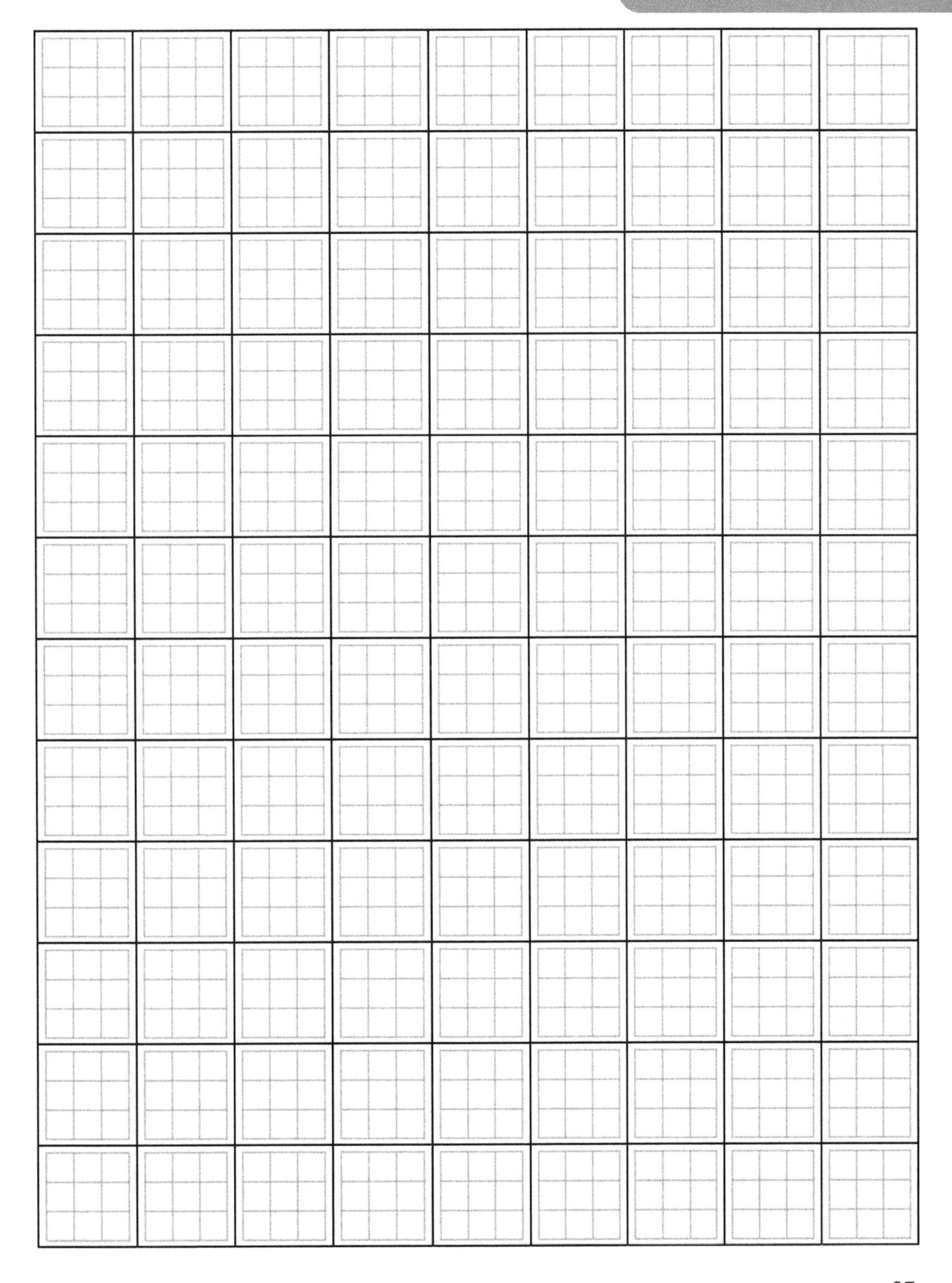

Practice Radicals

xīn heart 4 Strokes	心	**xīn** heart 3 Strokes	忄(V)					
gē spear 4 Strokes	戈							
hù door 4 Strokes	户	户 (V)						
shǒu hand 4 Strokes	手	**shǒu** hand 3 Strokes	扌(V)					
zhī branch 4 Strokes	支							
pū tap 4 Strokes	攴	攵 (V)						
wén script 4 Strokes	文							
dǒu dipper, vessel, measurer 4 Strokes	斗							
jīn axe 4 Strokes	斤							
fāng square 4 Strokes	方							
wú/ jì not 4 Strokes	无	旡 (V)						
rì sun 4 Strokes	日							

Self Practice

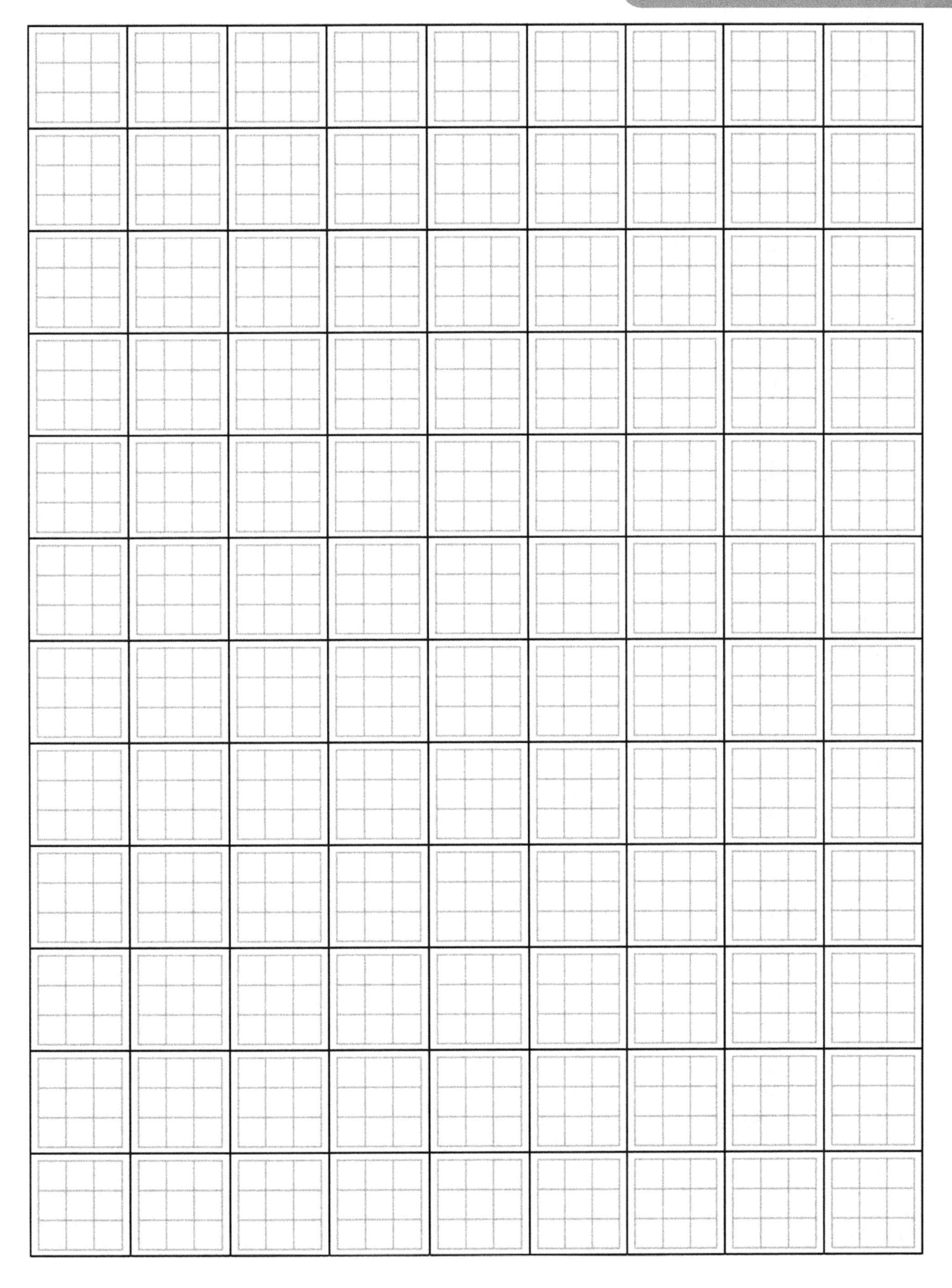

Practice Radicals

yuē say 4 Strokes	日							
yuè moon 4 Strokes	月							
mù tree 4 Strokes	木	木 (V)						
qiàn lack 4 Strokes	欠							
zhǐ stop 4 Strokes	止							
dǎi death 4 Strokes	歹							
shū weapon 4 Strokes	殳							
mǔ mother 5 Strokes	母	**mǔ** mother 4 Strokes	毋 (V)					
bǐ compare 4 Strokes	比							
máo fur 4 Strokes	毛							
shì clan 4 Strokes	氏							
qì steam 4 Strokes	气							

30

Self Practice

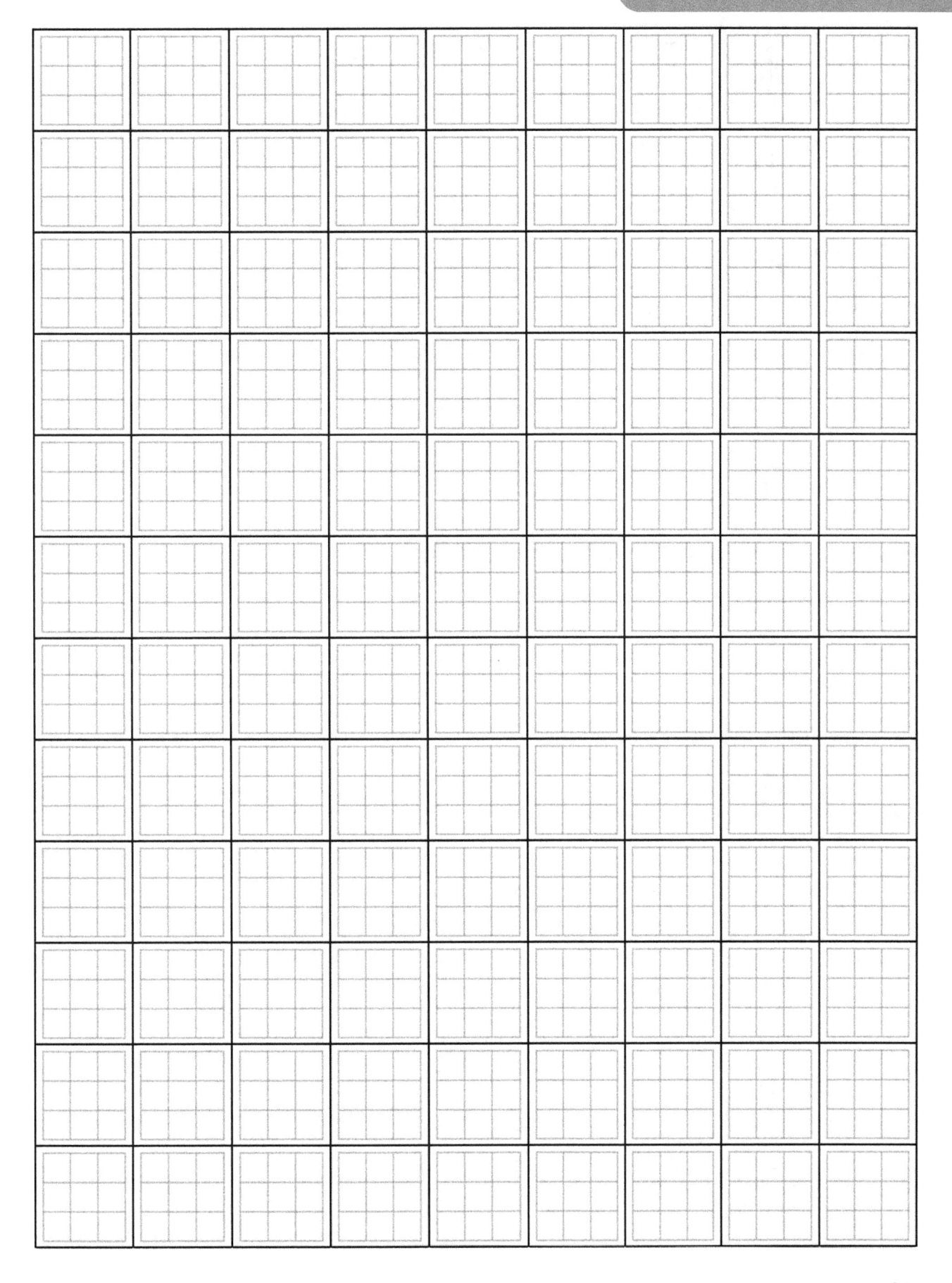

Practice Radicals

shuǐ water 4 Strokes	水	**shuǐ** water 3 Strokes	氵(V)	**shuǐ** water 5 Strokes	氺(V)				
huǒ fire 4 Strokes	火	(V) 灬							
zhǎo/zhuǎ claw 4 Strokes	爪	爫 (V)							
fù father 4 Strokes	父								
yáo Trigrams 4 Strokes	爻								
qiáng splitted, wood 4 Strokes	爿	**qiáng** splitted, wood 3 Strokes	丬(V)						
piàn slice 4 Strokes	片								
yá tooth 4 Strokes	牙								
niú cow 4 Strokes	牛	牛(V)	牛(V)						
quǎn dog 4 Strokes	犭	(V) 犬							
xuán profound 5 Strokes	玄								
wáng king 4 Strokes	王	**yù** jade 5 Strokes	玉(V)						

Self Practice

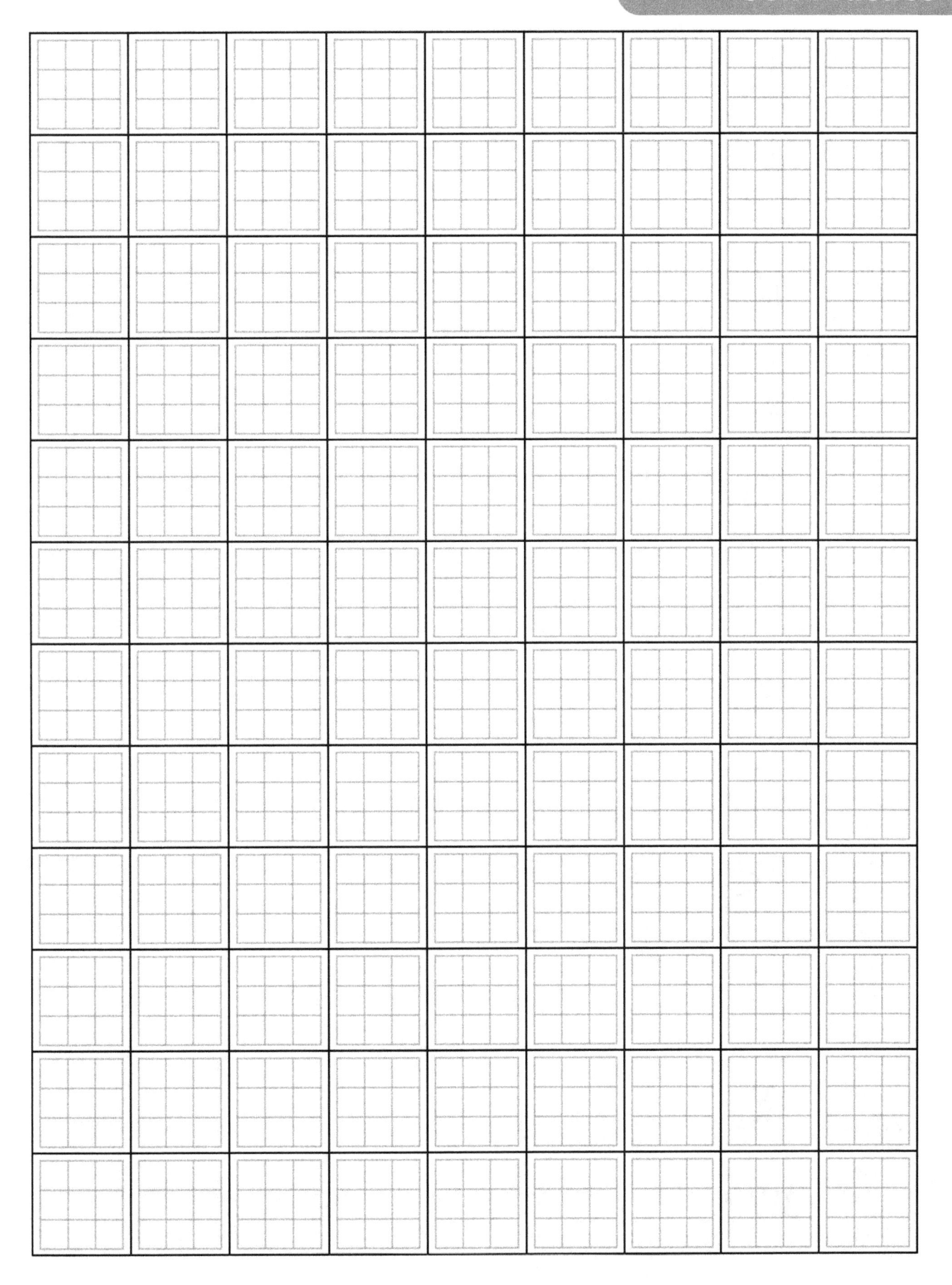

Practice Radicals

guā melon 5 Strokes	瓜								
wǎ tile 5 Strokes	瓦								
gān sweet 5 Strokes	甘								
shēng life 5 Strokes	生								
yòng use 5 Strokes	用								
tián field 5 Strokes	田								
pǐ bolt of cloth 5 Strokes	疋	疋 (V)							
nè sickness 5 Strokes	疒								
bō footsteps 5 Strokes	癶								
bái white 5 Strokes	白								
pí skin 5 Strokes	皮								
mǐn dish 5 Strokes	皿								

34

Self Practice

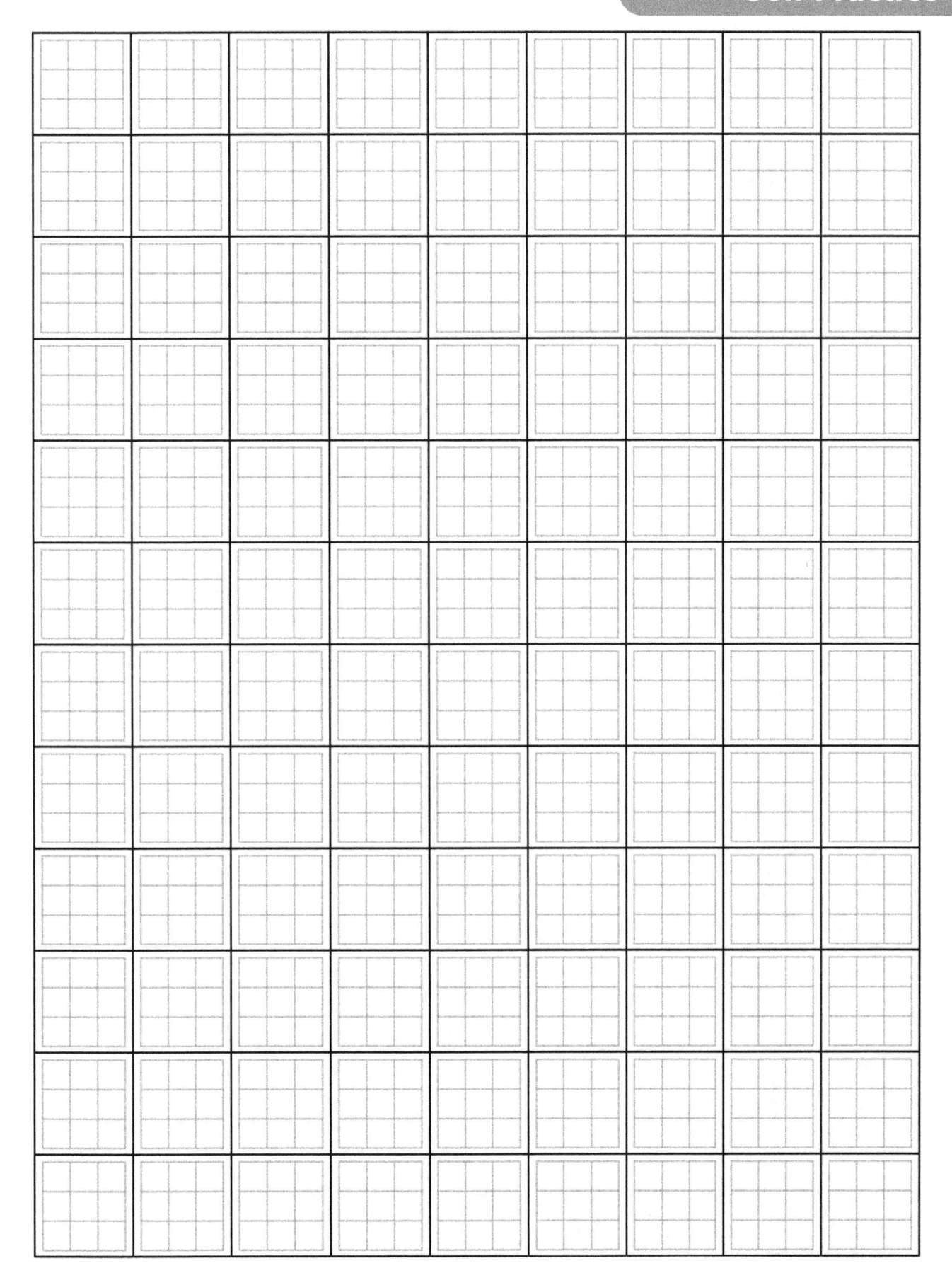

Practice Radicals

mù eye 5 Strokes	目							
máo spear 5 Strokes	矛							
shǐ arrow 5 Strokes	失							
shí stone 5 Strokes	石							
shì spirit 5 Strokes	示	**shì** spirit 4 Strokes	礻 (V)					
róu track 5 Strokes	禸							
hé grain 5 Strokes	禾							
xué cave 5 Strokes	穴							
lì stand 5 Strokes	立							
zhú bamboo 6 Strokes	竹	⺮ (V)	**zhú** bamboo 3 Strokes	⺮ (V)				
mǐ rice 6 Strokes	米							
mì silk 3 Strokes	纟	**mì** silk 6 Strokes	糸^(T)					

36

Self Practice

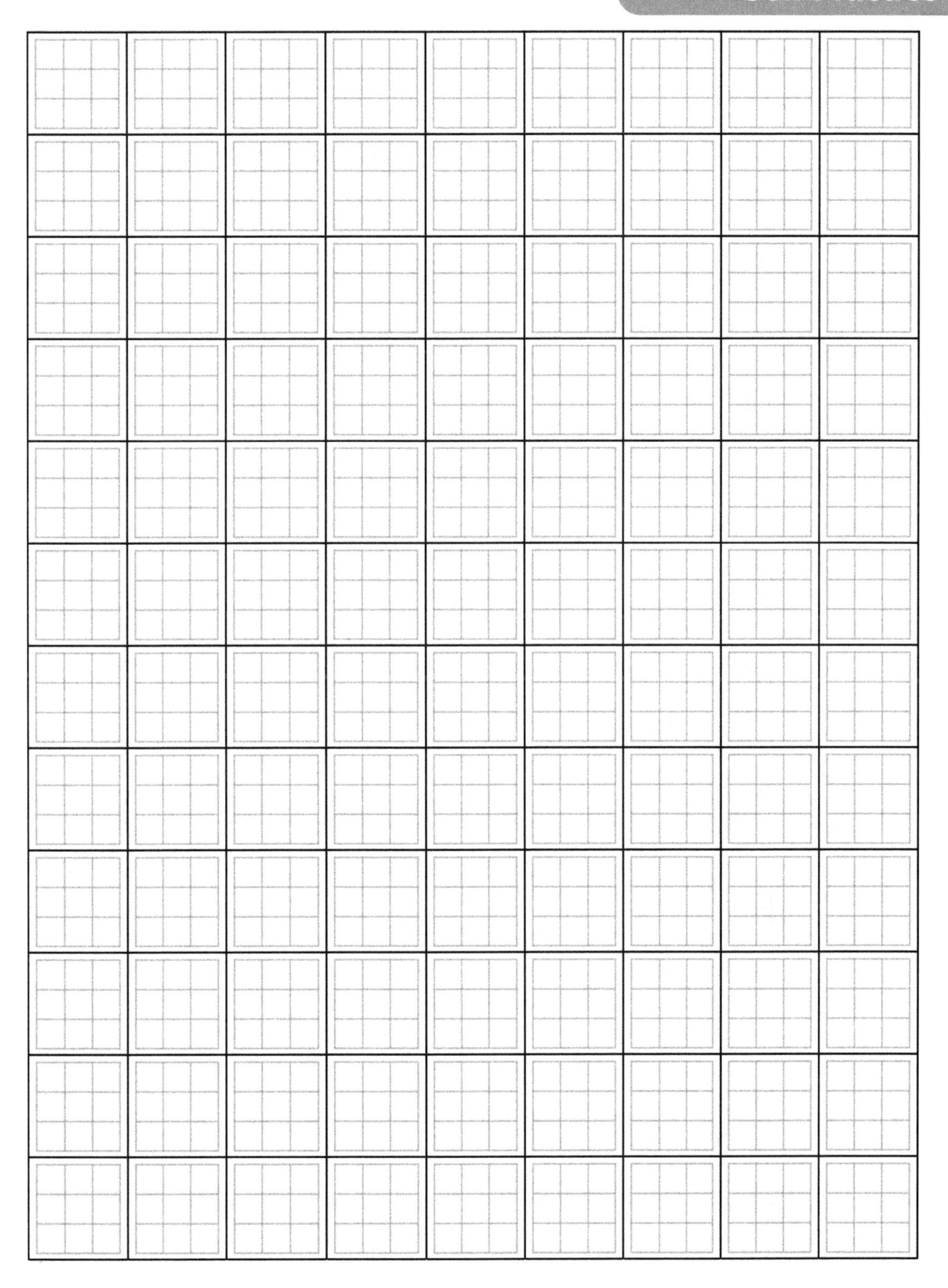

Practice Radicals

fǒu jar 6 Strokes	缶							
wǎng net 6 Strokes	网	**wǎng** net 4 Strokes	冈 (V)	**wǎng** net 5 Strokes	四 (V)			
yáng sheep 6 Strokes	羊	羊 (V)	羊 (V)					
yǔ feather 6 Strokes	羽							
lǎo old 6 Strokes	老	**lǎo** old 4 Strokes	耂 (V)					
ér and 6 Strokes	而							
lěi plow 6 Strokes	耒							
ěr ear 6 Strokes	耳							
yù brush 6 Strokes	聿							
ròu meat 6 Strokes	肉	**ròu** meat 4 Strokes	月 (V)					
chén minister 6 Strokes	臣							
zì self 6 Strokes	自							

Self Practice

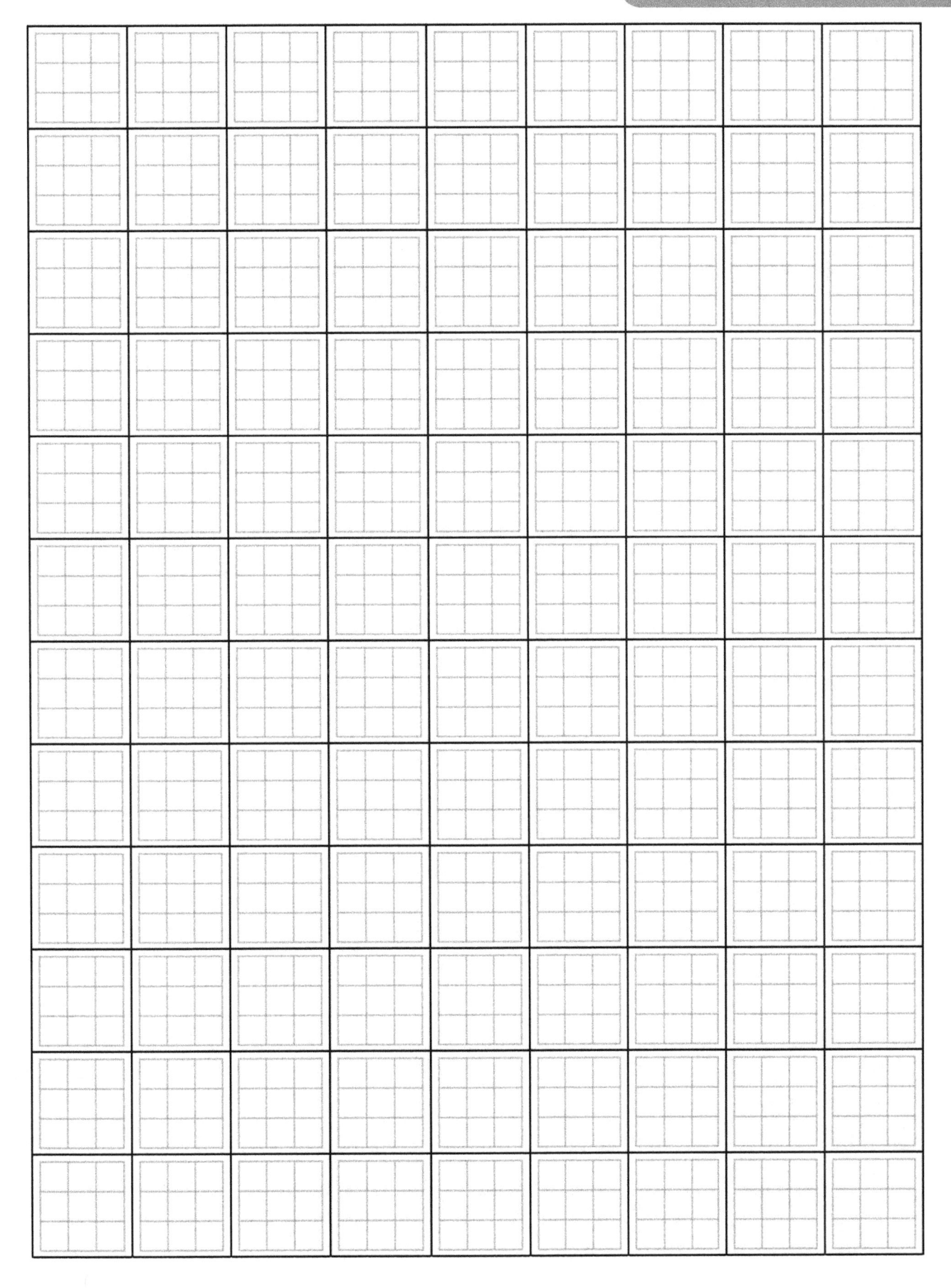

Practice Radicals

zhì arrive 6 Strokes	至								
jiù mortar 6 Strokes	臼								
shé tongue 6 Strokes	舌								
chuǎn oppose 6 Strokes	舛								
zhōu boat 6 Strokes	舟								
gèn stopping 6 Strokes	艮								
sè color 6 Strokes	色								
cǎo grass 6 Strokes	艸								
hū tiger 6 Strokes	虍								
chóng insect 6 Strokes	虫								
xuè blood 6 Strokes	血								
xíng walk 6 Strokes	行								

Self Practice

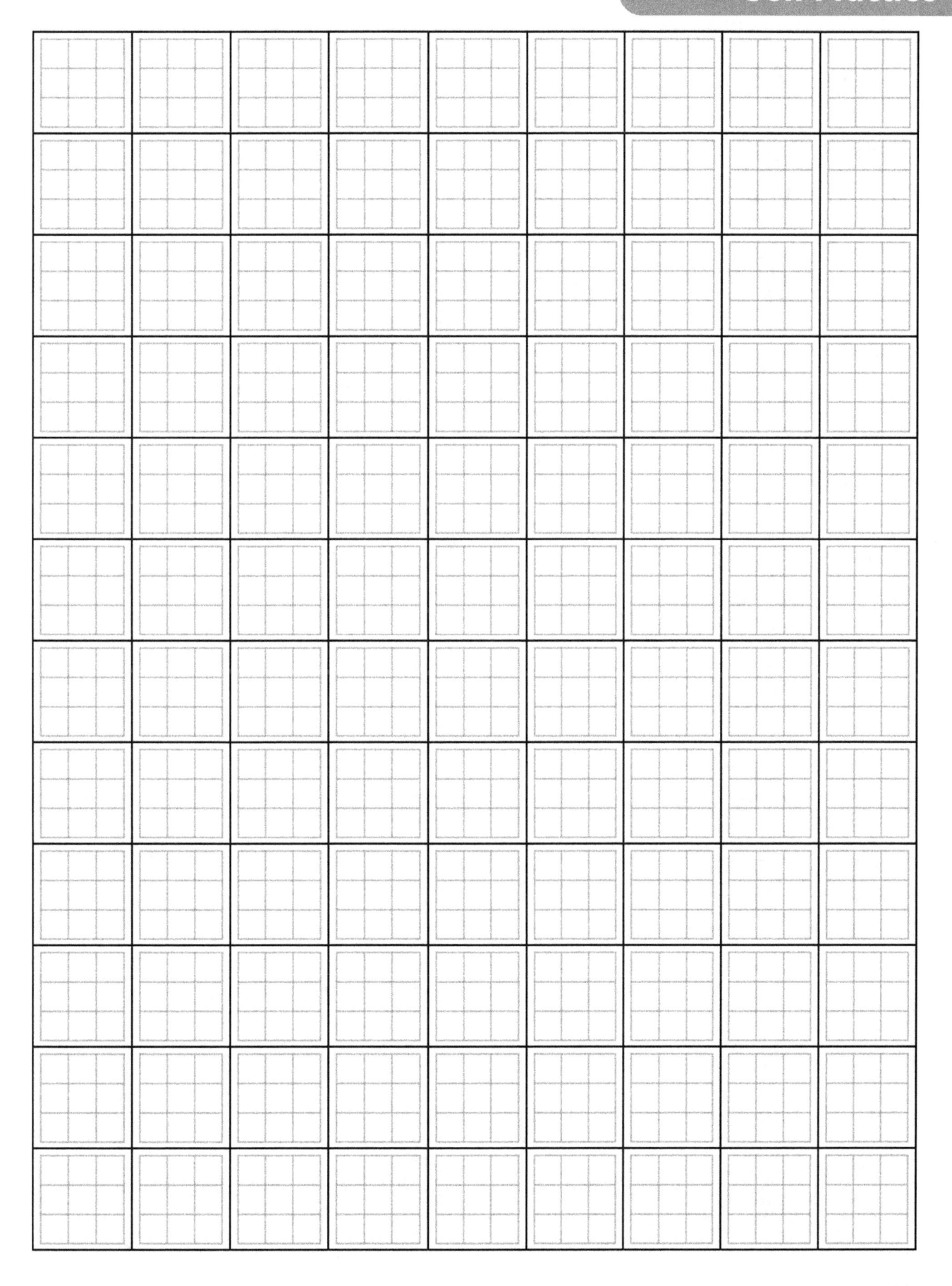

Practice Radicals

yī clothes 6 Strokes	衣	**yī** clothes 5 Strokes	衤(V)					
yà/ xī cover, west 6 Strokes	西	西(V)						
jiàn see 4 Strokes	见	**jiàn** see 7 Strokes	見(T)					
jiǎo horn 7 Strokes	角							
yán speech 2 Strokes	讠	**yán** speech 7 Strokes	言(T)					
gǔ valley 7 Strokes	谷							
dòu bean 7 Strokes	豆							
shǐ pig 7 Strokes	豕							
zhì badger 7 Strokes	豸							
bèi shell 4 Strokes	贝	**bèi** shell 7 Strokes	貝(T)					
chì red 7 Strokes	赤							
zǒu run 7 Strokes	走							

Self Practice

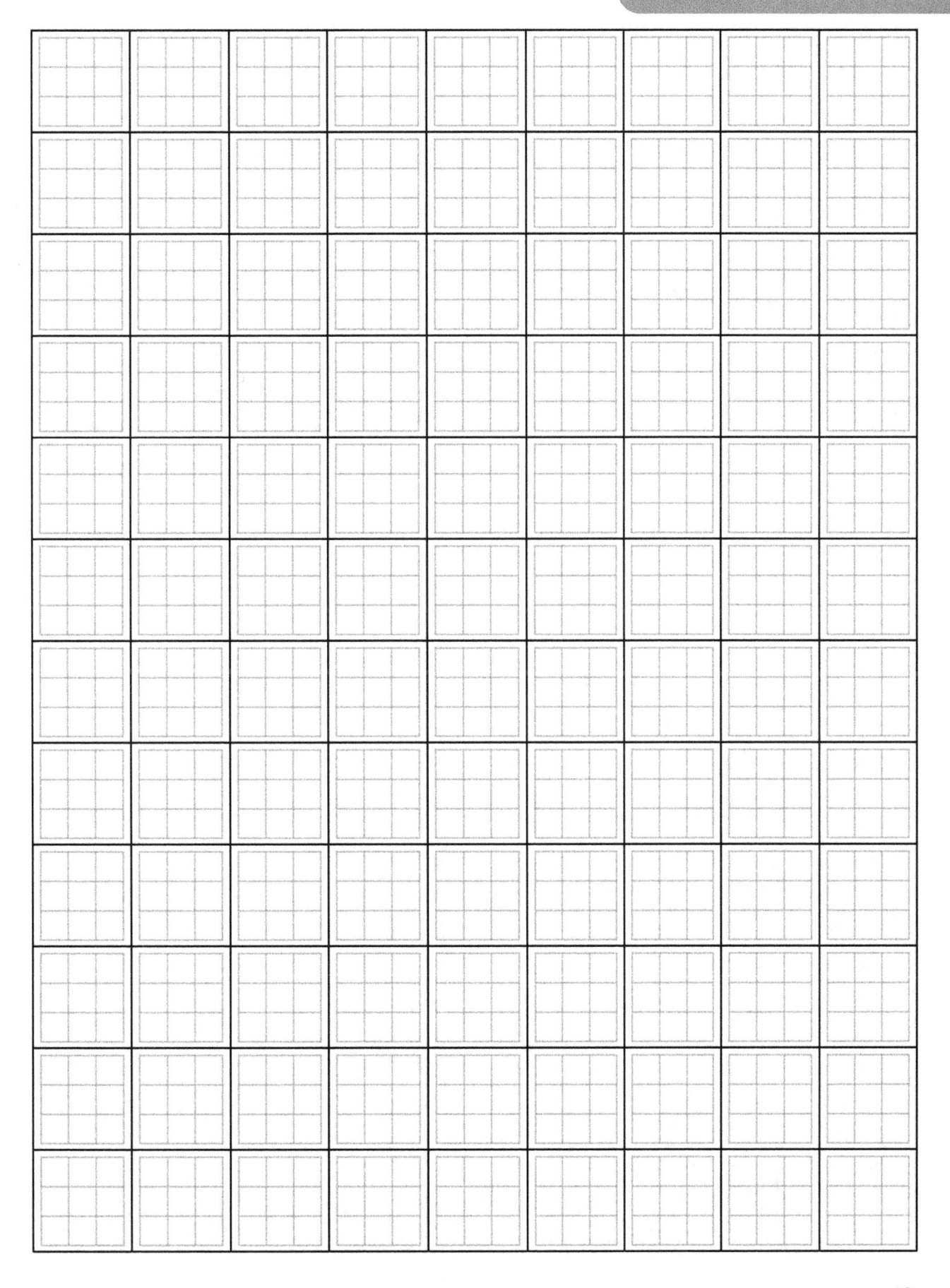

Practice Radicals

zú foot 7 Strokes	足		
shēn body 7 Strokes	身		
chē cart 4 Strokes	车	**chē** cart 7 Strokes	車 (T)
xīn bitter 7 Strokes	辛		
chén morning 7 Strokes	辰		
chuò walk 7 Strokes	辵		
yì city 7 Strokes	邑	**yì** city 2 Strokes	阝 (V)
yǒu wine 7 Strokes	酉		
biàn distinguish 7 Strokes	采		
lǐ village 7 Strokes	里		
jīn gold, metal 5 Strokes	钅	**jīn** gold, metal 8 Strokes	金 (V)
cháng long 4 Strokes	长	**cháng** long 8 Strokes	長 (T)

44

Self Practice

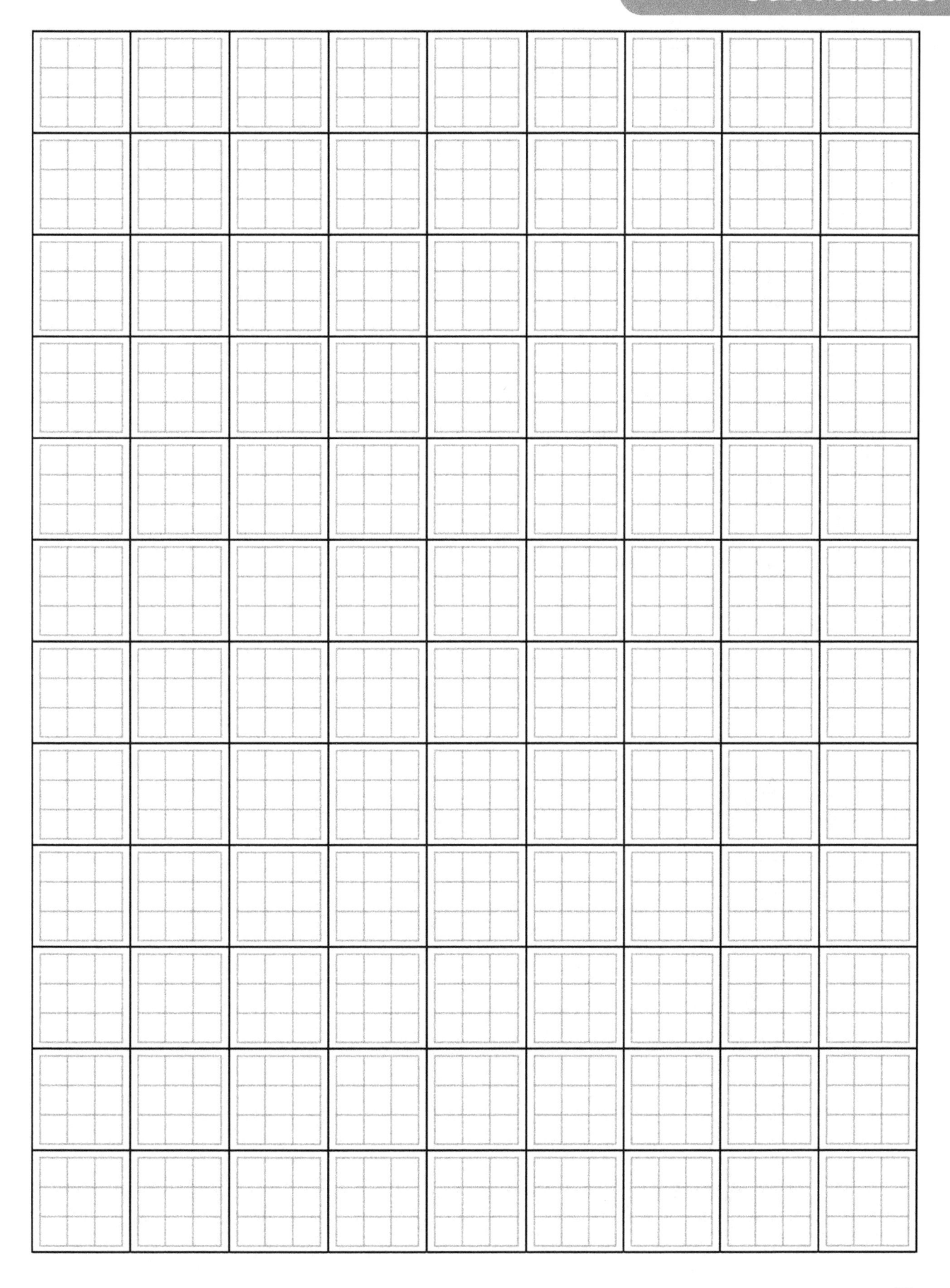

Practice Radicals

mén gate 3 Strokes	门	**mén** gate 8 Strokes	門 (V)					
fù mound 8 Strokes	阜	**fù** mound 2 Strokes	阝 (V)					
lì slave 8 Strokes	隶							
zhuī small bird 8 Strokes	隹							
yǔ rain 8 Strokes	雨							
qīng blue 8 Strokes	青							
fēi wrong 8 Strokes	非							
miàn face 9 Strokes	面							
gé leather 9 Strokes	革							
wéi tanned leather 4 Strokes	韦	**wéi** tanned leather 9 Strokes	韋 (T)					
jiǔ leek 9 Strokes	韭							
yīn sound 9 Strokes	音							

Self Practice

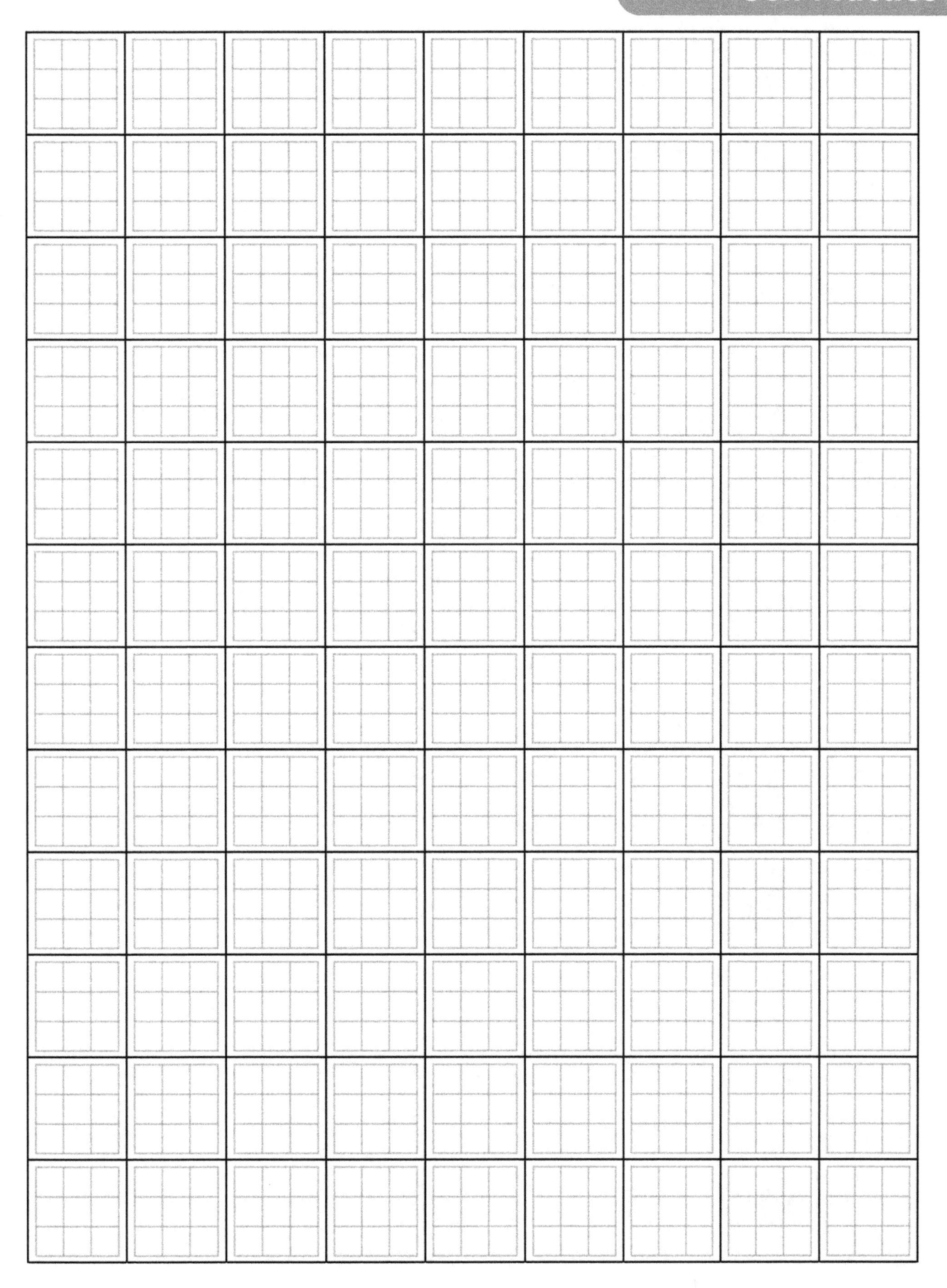

Practice Radicals

yè leaf/page 6 Strokes	页	yè leaf/page 8 Strokes	頁 (T)
fēng wind 4 Strokes	风	fēng wind 9 Strokes	風 (T)
fēi* fly 3 Strokes	飞	fēi fly 9 Strokes	飛 (T)
shí eat 9 Strokes	食	shí eat 8 Strokes	飠 (V) / shí eat 3 Strokes 饣 (V)
shǒu head 9 Strokes	首		
xiāng fragrant 9 Strokes	香		
mǎ horse 3 Strokes	马	mǎ horse 9 Strokes	馬 (T)
gǔ bone 10 Strokes	骨		
gāo tall 10 Strokes	高		
biāo hair 10 Strokes	髟		
dòu * fight 10 Strokes	鬥		
chàng * sacrificial wine 10 Strokes	鬯		

48

Self Practice

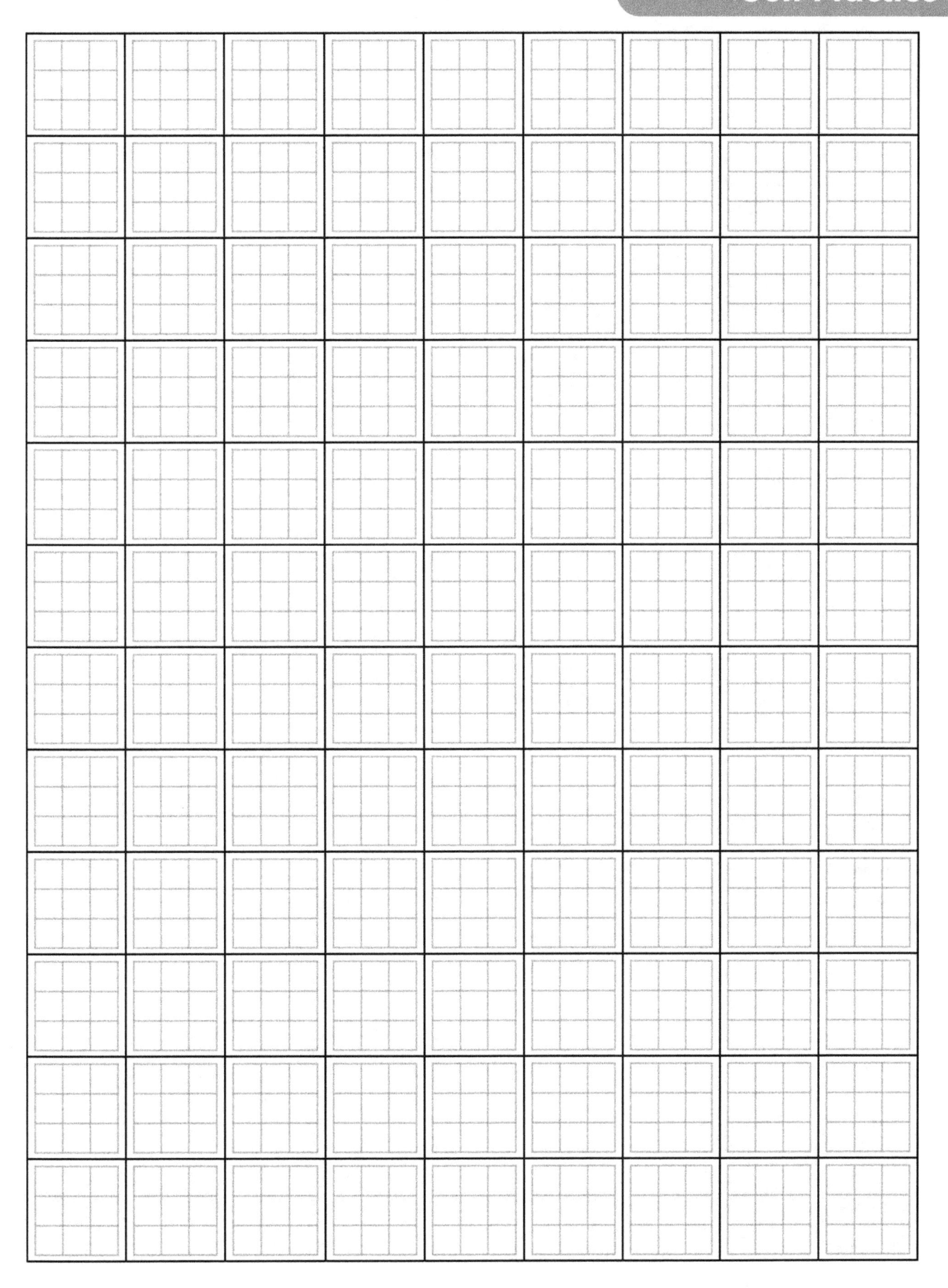

Practice Radicals

lì cauldron 10 Strokes	鬲								
guǐ ghost 10 Strokes	鬼								
yú fish 8 Strokes	鱼	**yú** fish 11 Strokes	魚 (T)						
niǎo bird 5 Strokes	鸟	**niǎo** bird 11 Strokes	鳥 (T)						
lǔ salt 11 Strokes	卤								
lù deer 11 Strokes	鹿								
mài wheat 7 Strokes	麦	**mài** wheat 11 Strokes	麥 (T)						
má hemp 11 Strokes	麻								
huáng yellow 12 Strokes	黄								
shǔ * millet 12 Strokes	黍								
hēi black 12 Strokes	黑								
zhǐ * embroidery 12 Strokes	黹								

Self Practice

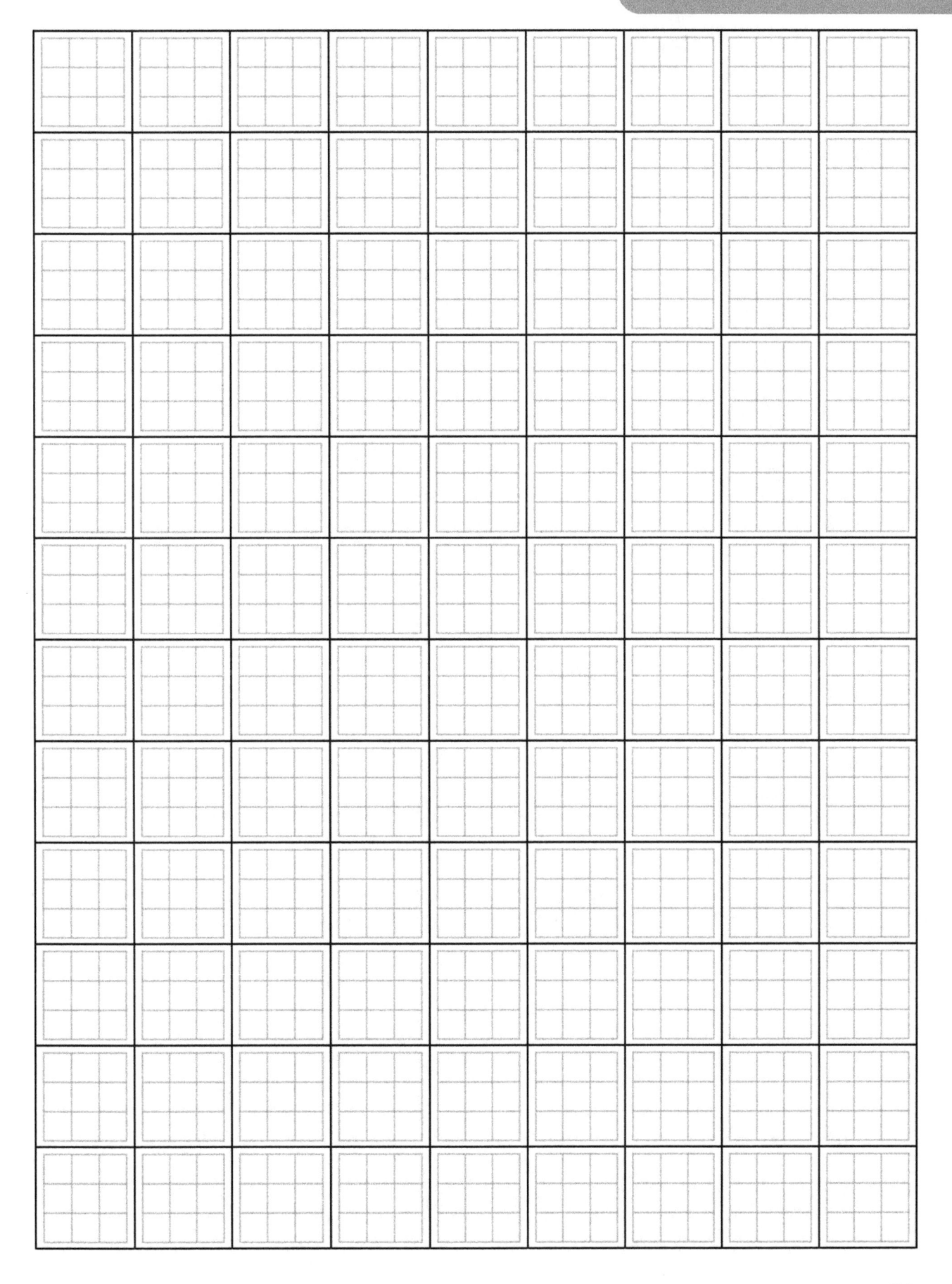

Practice Radicals

mǐn frog 8 Strokes	黾	mǐn frog 13 Strokes	黽 (T)
dǐng * tripod 13 Strokes	鼎		
gǔ drum 13 Strokes	鼓		
shǔ rat 13 Strokes	鼠		
bí nose 14 Strokes	鼻		
qí even 6 Strokes	齐	qí even 14 Strokes	齊 (T)
chǐ tooth 8 Strokes	齿	chǐ tooth 15 Strokes	齒 (T)
lóng dragon 5 Strokes	龙	lóng dragon 16 Strokes	龍 (T)
guī turtle 7 Strokes	龟	guī turtle 16 Strokes	龜 (T)
yuè flute 17 Strokes	龠		

52

Self Practice

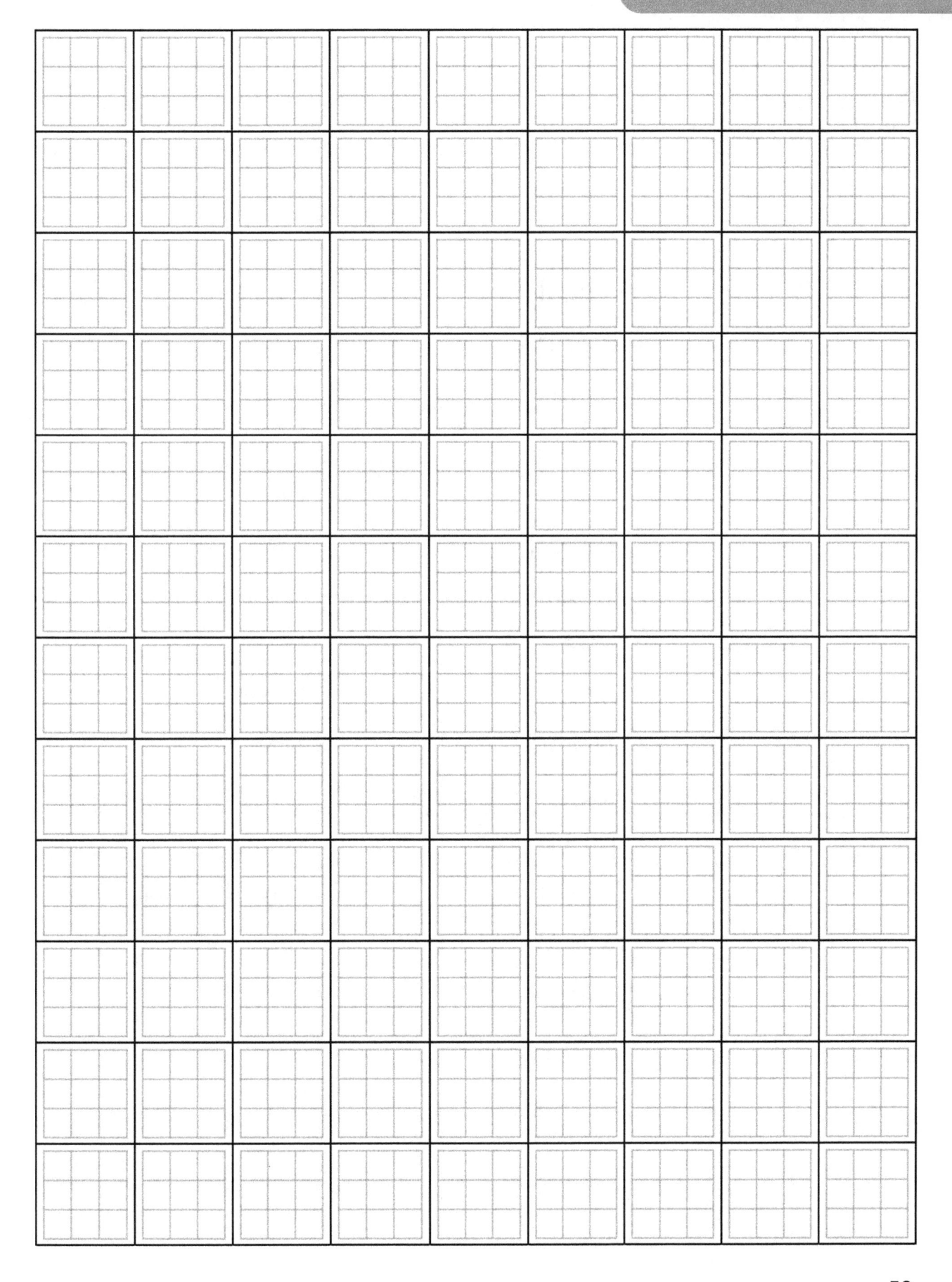

Typical Characters

Practice the following words and see if you can identify the radical by utilizing your knowledge of radicals:

磨	[mó]	to polish
绳	[shéng]	rope
鲜	[xiān]	fresh
滑	[huá]	to slip
道	[dào]	path
疯	[fēng]	crazy
罪	[zuì]	crime
谁	[shéi]	who?
问	[wèn]	to ask
钱	[qián]	money
话	[huà]	to speak
街	[jiē]	street
姥	[lǎo]	maternal grandmother
位	[wèi]	position/ rank
冰	[bīng]	ice/ ice-cold
打	[dǎ]	to hit
学	[xué]	to study

Self Practice

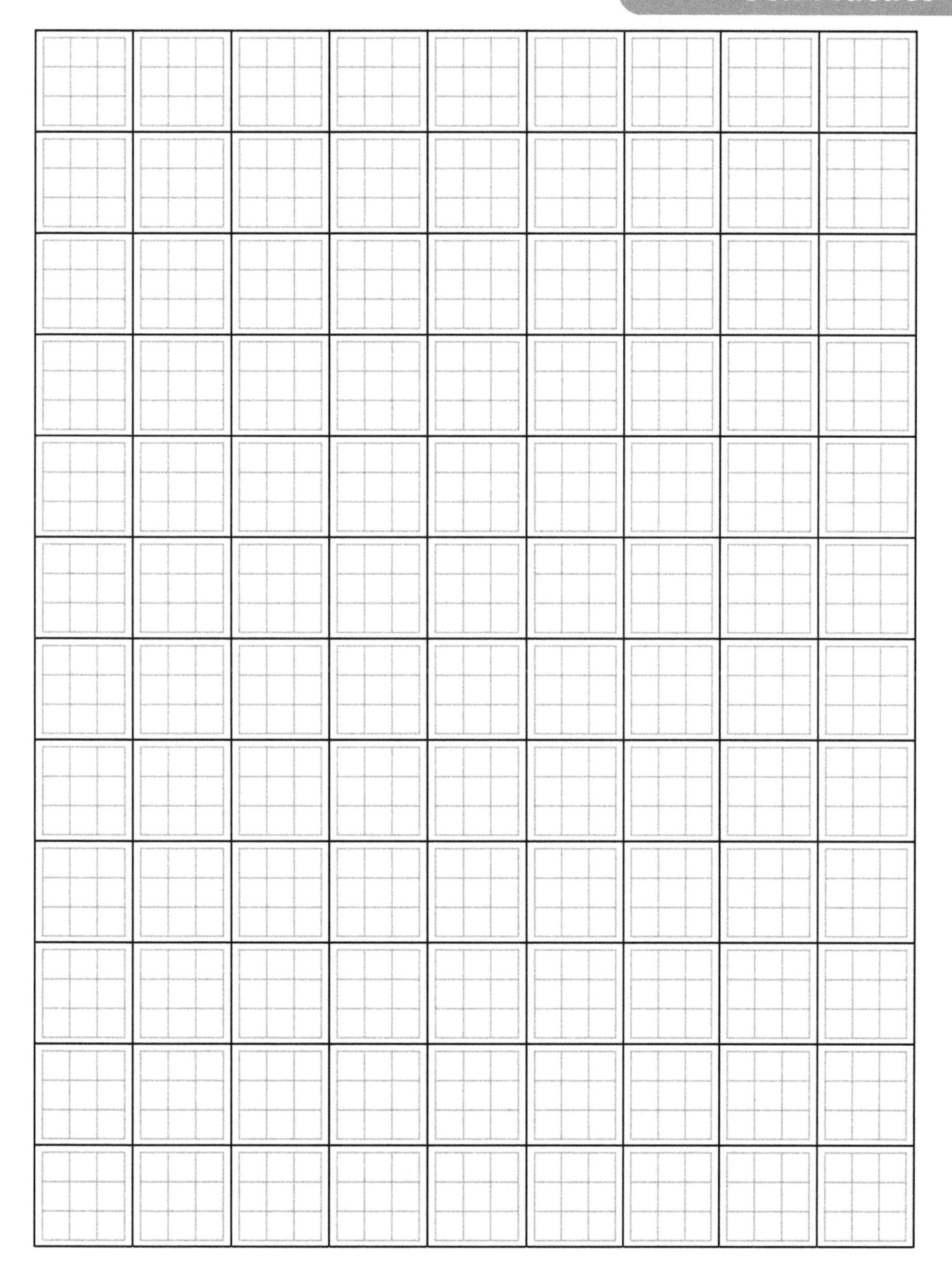

Self Practice

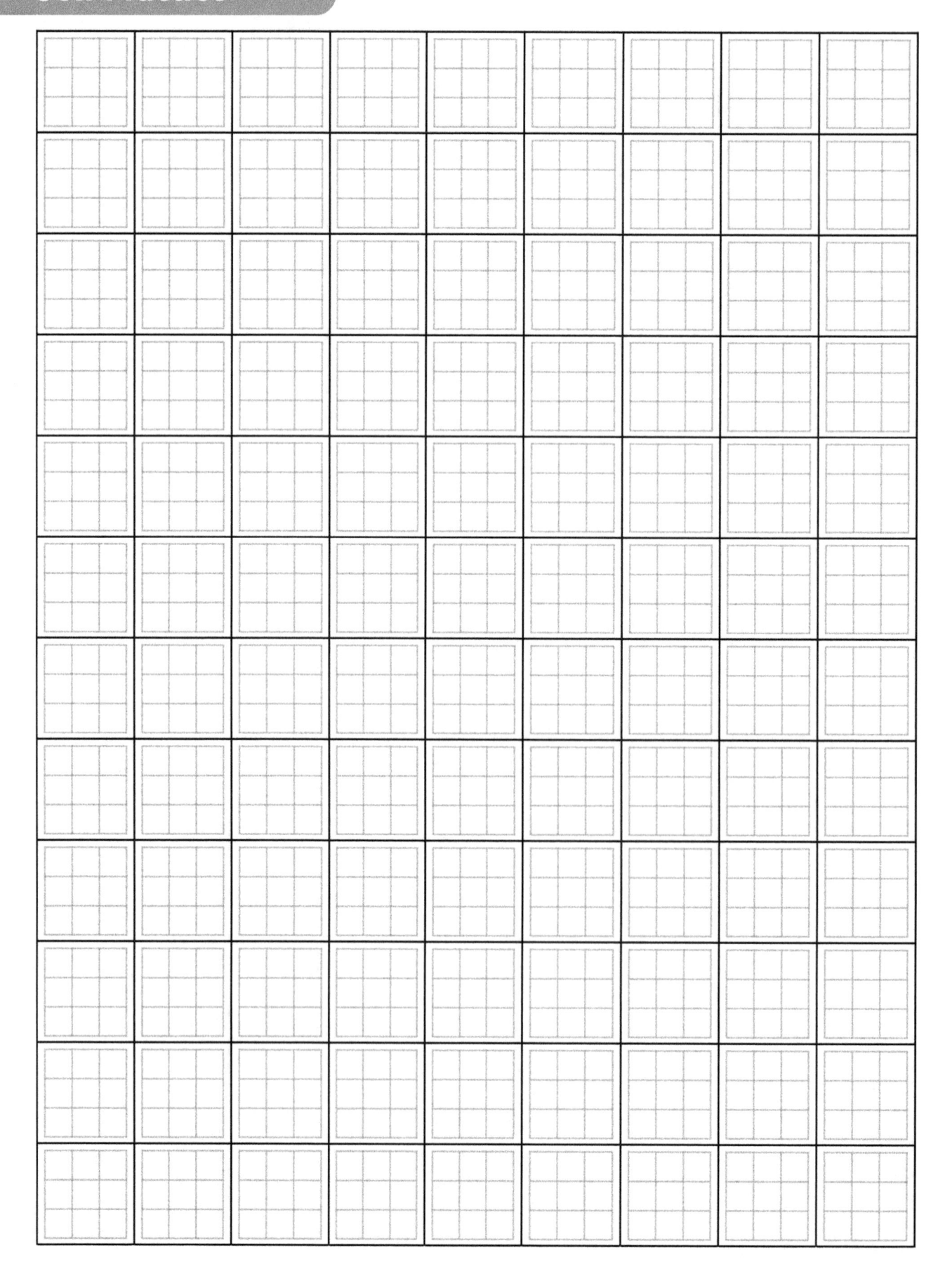

Self Practice

Self Practice

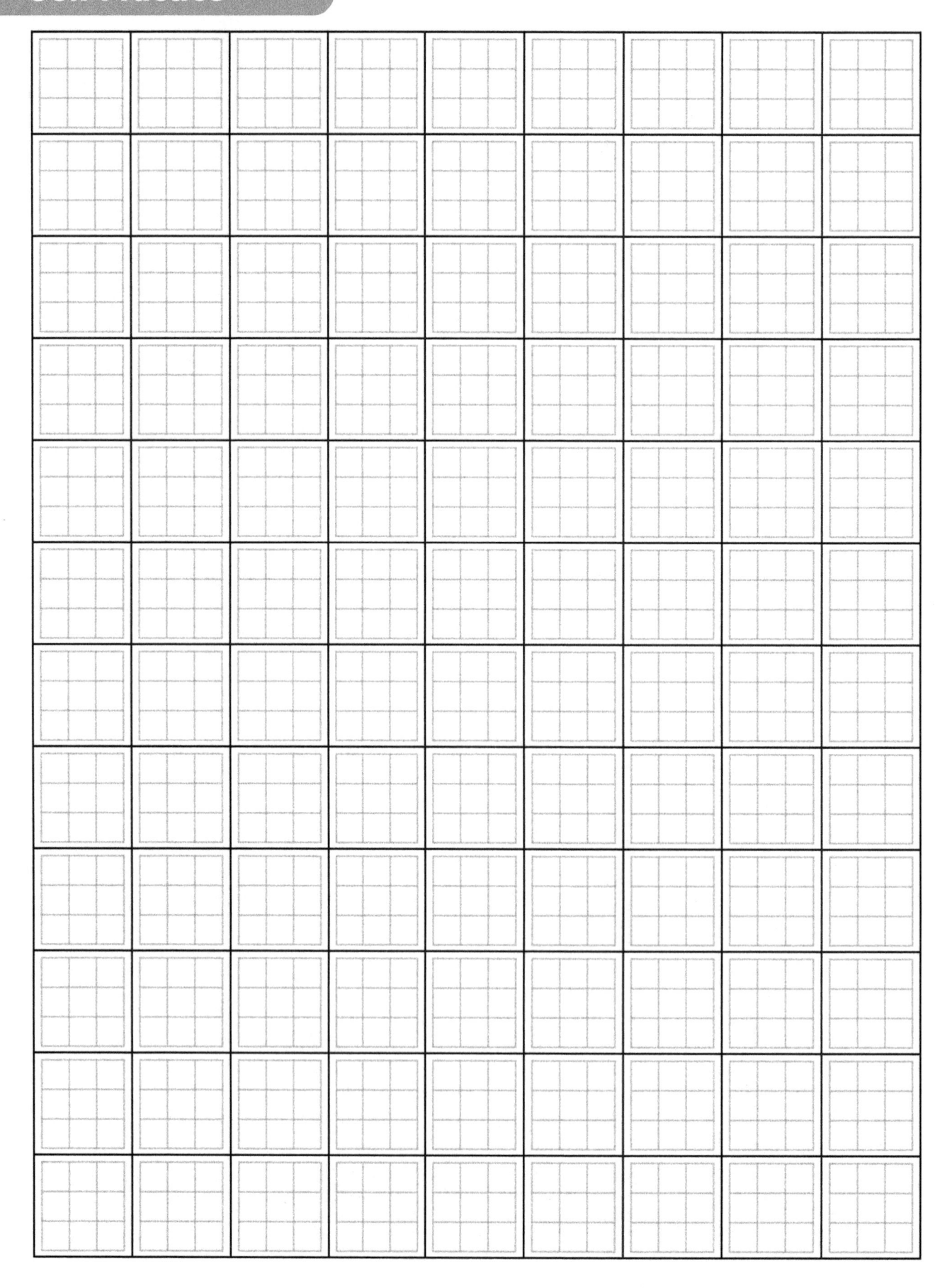

Self Practice

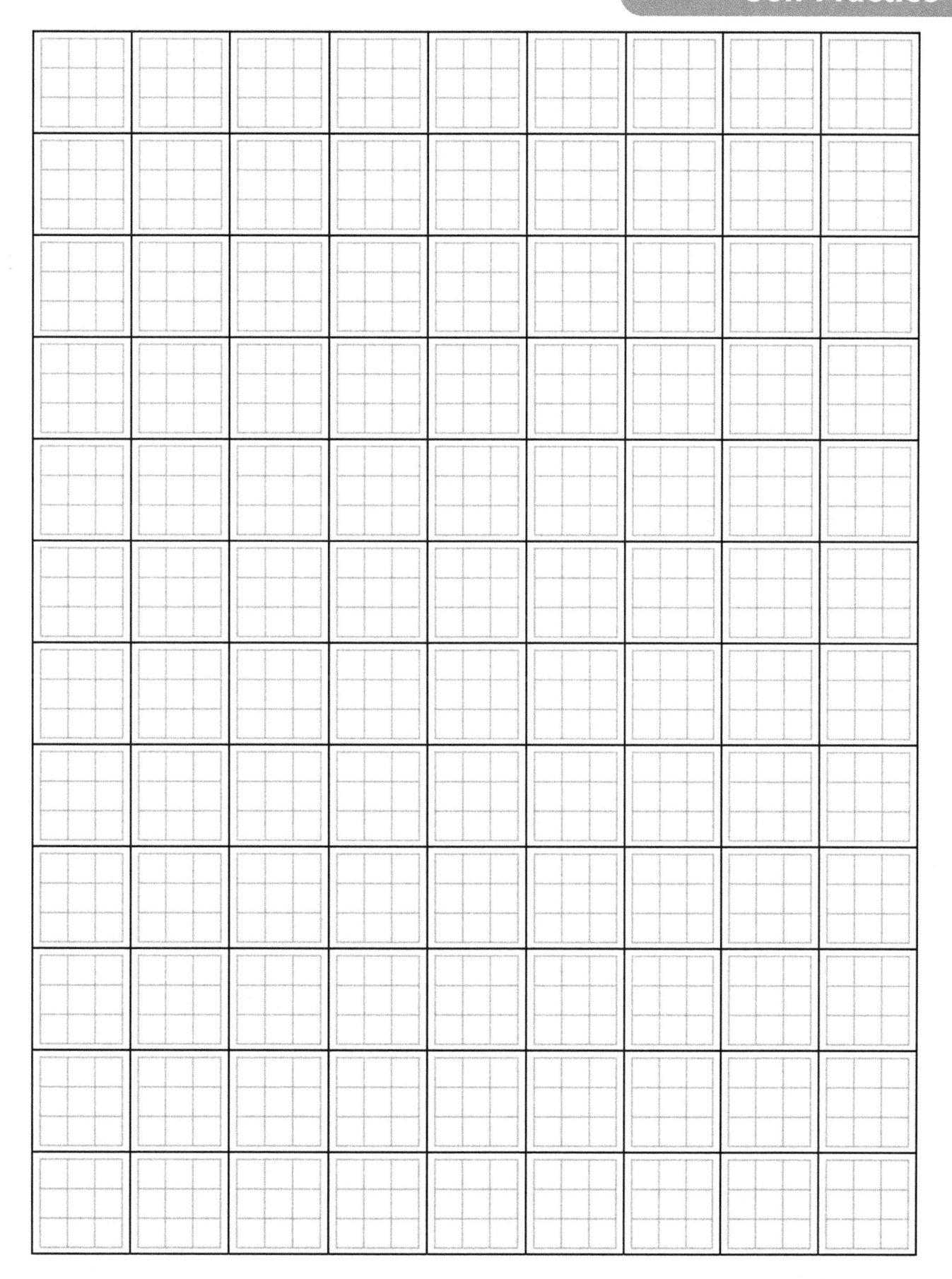